ONE-TRACK MIND

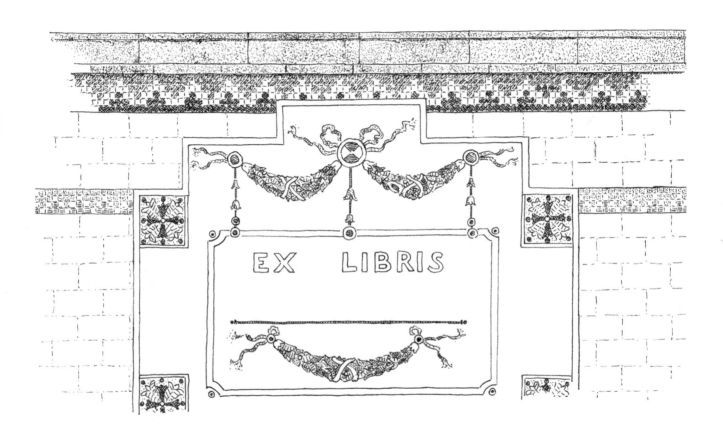

EX LIBRIS

ONE-TRACK MIND

DRAWING THE NEW YORK SUBWAY

Drawings by
PHILIP ASHFORTH COPPOLA

Foreword by
JONATHAN LETHEM

Edited by
EZRA BOOKSTEIN & JEREMY WORKMAN

PRINCETON ARCHITECTURAL PRESS

NEW YORK

Published by
Princeton Architectural Press
A McEvoy Group company
202 Warren Street
Hudson, New York 12534
Visit our website at www.papress.com

Princeton Architectural Press is a leading publisher
in architecture, design, photography, landscape,
and visual culture. We create fine books and
stationery of unsurpassed quality and production
values. With more than one thousand titles
published, we find design everywhere and in the
most unlikely places.

All artwork by Philip Ashforth Coppola. The text
contains material adapted from *Silver Connections*
by Philip Ashforth Coppola © 2013. Reprinted with
permission of the author.

Every reasonable attempt has been made to
identify owners of copyright. Errors or omissions
will be corrected in subsequent editions. All efforts
have been made to ensure factual accuracy; any
inaccuracies that remain are the responsibility
of the authors.

Editor: Nina Pick
Design: Jan Haux
Typesetting: Paul Wagner

Special thanks to: Ryan Alcazar, Janet Behning,
Nolan Boomer, Abby Bussel, Benjamin English,
Jan Cigliano Hartman, Susan Hershberg,
Kristen Hewitt, Lia Hunt, Valerie Kamen,
Jennifer Lippert, Sara McKay, Eliana Miller,
Wes Seeley, Rob Shaeffer, Sara Stemen,
Marisa Tesoro, and Joseph Weston of
Princeton Architectural Press
—Kevin C. Lippert, publisher

Library of Congress
Cataloging-in-Publication Data
Names: Coppola, Philip Ashforth, author, artist.
   | Workman, Jeremy, editor. | Bookstein, Ezra,
   editor. | Lethem, Jonathan, writer of foreword.
Title: One-track mind : drawing the New York
   subway / drawings by Philip Ashforth Coppola ;
   Jeremy Workman and Ezra Bookstein, editors ;
   foreword by Jonathan Lethem.
Description: First edition. | New York : Princeton
   Architectural Press, 2018. | Contains material
   adapted from Silver Connections by Philip
   Ashforth Coppola.
Identifiers: LCCN 2017037147 | ISBN 9781616896744
   (alk. paper)
Subjects: LCSH: Subways—New York (State)—New
   York. | Subways—Decoration—New York (State)—
   New York.
Classification: LCC TF847.N5 C582 2018 | DDC
   741.973—dc23
LC record available at https://lccn.loc
   .gov/2017037147

TABLE OF CONTENTS

FOREWORD

I remember one day, during my short-lived participation in the Music and Art High School soccer team, going north from Manhattan after school, the direction I'd never otherwise go, to Van Cortlandt Park in the Bronx for practice. (I lived in Brooklyn and traveled to Harlem every day for school on the A train.) We were having dinner that night with friends who lived in Staten Island, and it occurred to me, on the subway headed south, that if I diverted to Queens on my way to the dinner and dropped in on my grandmother in Sunnyside, I'd have hit all five boroughs in one day. This act may be routine for marathon runners and mayoral candidates, but it gave me a little shiver of completist satisfaction to do it.

I remember, also during high school, my friends and I finding fresh Keith Haring chalk drawings on the empty black billboard frames in the 135th Street station and smearing them with our hands and laughing about it. We saw the Haring drawings all through the system those days, and we resented him a little for it, in our brat-punk way; we resented him simply for having been there before us, for seeming to be everywhere.

I remember Darius McCollum, who spent his teenage years and beyond impersonating NYC transit workers and illegally driving trains, and got himself sent to Rikers Island for doing so. And I remember Keron Thomas, who at sixteen practiced for months for a single remarkable three-hour joyride as a fake motorman on the A train, one in which he successfully transported thousands of New Yorkers to their destinations with barely a hitch.

I remember the first time I really noticed the Astor Place beaver mosaic, like so many before me have done and are likely doing right at this moment, and marveled at New York's capacity to persistently disgorge secrets hidden in plain sight, lost histories in ruins and still a part of the (barely) functioning infrastructure, the eccentric system of public trains, which had actually arisen as two rival private rail systems, and which everyone took for granted as if it had grown there, a natural formation, and which most people only complain about or silently endure. I remember trying to conjugate that beaver mosaic with the name of the station and with the portion of the city above—I was surely visiting to go to some Astor Place club, or teenage party—and failing. Could there actually have been a beaver dam at that site in living human memory? And if so, why would it be commemorated in the station's tilework?

You may ask, now, why on earth would I compare these inadequate and fitful and irreverent and even illegal expressions of surplus fascination with the New York subway system with the titanic accomplishments of the great self-appointed scholar and copyist of the system's decorations, Philip Ashforth Coppola? Coppola, who with saintly intensity has burrowed into the fading archives, dwelling there for decades now like Kafka's creature from "The Burrow," recording and tracing that which speaks to him at a level deeper than most could imagine? Coppola, whose hand and breath and presence are like those of a dutiful ghost, so that he passes largely unseen, claiming no glory for himself, only enlivening and illuminating the darkening record, the accomplishments of men who passed before our time and who were likely, even willing, to be forgotten? Why, I might as well compare him to a graffiti artist!

Well, I'll do that too. In one sense, sure, a graffiti artist is Coppola's exact opposite—a defacer, a proclaimer, an impulse artist. Yet, like some of the other forms of subway obsessives I've mentioned, I think the NYC graffiti artist's desire arises from a similar place, from the urge to find a way to talk back, whether in a whisper or a scream, to the great secret system of the subways. For the New York subways are like a magical nervous system, or a secret, vastly distributed spare brain, which every serious New Yorker understands has the power to speak to him or her in a mythic voice, even if one chooses to ignore it. It might be a great burden, this listening; we might only choose to do it momentarily, or to call it to a halt after a certain unbearable intensity has been reached, and cry "Enough!" Well, here might be a good-enough description of Phil Coppola: he is the voice's greatest listener, the mystery's greatest detective. He is the man who never cried "Enough!" Like a character from Borges, his impossible *Silver Connections* project proposes

a map that is the exact size of the
territory it describes. Most of us
can only envy an artist, and a life, as
unwavering and pure.

—*Jonathan Lethem*

INTRODUCTION

If you've been in a New York City subway station sometime in the past forty years, you may have passed by him. The guy staring off at a mosaic on the wall, painstakingly sketching each of its tiles into a cheap spiral notebook, is Phillip Ashforth Coppola.

In 1978, after noticing that the original mosaics in the Bowling Green subway station and the ferry boat tiles of the Cortland Street station had been removed and destroyed during renovation, Philip Ashforth Coppola set out to create an encyclopedia of the design and decorative elements of every station in the system before they too vanished. It was to be the definitive story of the overlooked mosaics, plaques, relief sculptures, and modeled faience that were designed to showcase the new subway system as part of the Gilded Age's City Beautiful movement. Coppola's goal was to immortalize this art and try to identify the forgotten craftsmen, artisans, and designers who produced it. He dedicated his weeknights and weekends to scouring the city's historical libraries for books, maps, directories, and turn-of-the-century newspapers, as well as riding from station to station with sketchbook in hand. Coppola would go on to spend the next four decades researching, writing, illustrating, self-funding, and self-publishing his encyclopedia, which he titled *Silver Connections*. Intended as a single book, it grew to six illustrated volumes totaling nearly two thousand pages, and though his plan is to include every station (there are 472 currently), Coppola has made it through only 110. Now seventy years old, he's still working on it; he hopes to finish his project by the mid-2030s.

Coppola's love of the subway began when he was a young boy. Born in East Orange, New Jersey, he grew up in the leafy suburb of Maplewood. When he was eight years old, his father, an accountant in Western Union's tax department, casually mentioned that down in the subway stations "there are pictures of old New York on the station walls." This comment seared into Coppola's mind, becoming the spark that would lead him on his lifelong path.

Coppola graduated from his local high school, briefly attended Rhode Island School of Design, and dreamed of a life as an artist. But his dreams didn't coalesce into an artistic career, at least not in the conventional sense. Aside from a two-year stint in Manhattan in the early 1970s, working an entry-level job at a publishing house, he lived most of his adult life in his childhood home with his mother, where he settled into a modest life as a printing-press operator, making letterheads, envelopes, and business cards.

A quiet and humble man, Coppola didn't attract attention. In the early years, he was often dismissed by subway historians as just another "foamer" (the derisive term for subway fans who "foam at the mouth" from excitement). His first volume, self-published in 1984, was ignored by scholars and librarians, as few recognized the scope of his research or talent of his artistry. But little by little, by the late 1990s, local transit historians began to whisper about *Silver Connections*—"Have you seen it?" "They say he's sketched every mosaic!" "Is it real?"—and word of its magnitude spread. Some wondered if Coppola himself was another modern-day Joe Gould—the central character in Joseph Mitchell's famous *New Yorker* profile whose long-gestating book proved to be nonexistent. Coppola's seller, New York Bound Books, was an early champion of his work. However, they struggled to get the book on shelves, so only the lucky few ever saw it. Copies were scarce (roughly nine hundred volumes have been sold in over three decades), but *Silver Connections* eventually attained legendary status within those very circles of New York City which had previously locked him out. The *New York Times* keeps a copy in their research room. The New York Transit Museum keeps one as well.

But Coppola's work is much more than an exhaustive study of the subway's history and artwork; *Silver Connections'* true gift is his meticulously hand-drawn illustrations—the New York subway's very own illuminated manuscript.

Each of his drawings takes days of work. Coppola begins "on site" on a subway platform sketching in his trusty notebook (there are forty-one of them to date), then returns home to draw the mosaics anew with the most basic of a draftsman's tools: a sheet of paper, a ruler, and a pen.

The six volumes to date include hundreds of his black-and-white illustrations. With each drawing, Coppola preserves a glimpse of that golden age of optimism, when the Gilded Age was ushering in "the future" right before New Yorkers' eyes; when, on March 24, 1900, twenty-five thousand people packed City Hall Park to witness the subway system's ground breaking and the wonders it promised.

Part outsider artist, part master draftsman, part preservationist, Philip Ashforth Coppola, with this book, takes his rightful place as an artist of distinct and unique talent. Equally important, this book serves his original goal of bringing attention to the subway's long forgotten artists and craftspeople. Hopefully it can also remind New Yorker and visitor alike that there is beauty all around us. You just have to look.

—Ezra Bookstein and Jeremy Workman, 2018

THE BIRTH OF THE NEW YORK CITY SUBWAY

At the time of the New York subway system's conception, as the nineteenth century was coming to a close, the city had a handful of privately operated, steam-powered, elevated trains. They were standalone endeavors, in competition with each other, constantly going into and out of bankruptcy. The subway was to be a marvel of public transportation that would finally unite the city. Furthermore, it would embody the ideals and monumental grandeur of America's new City Beautiful movement, which in New York would also give birth to the main public library and post office, Pennsylvania Station, and the new Grand Central Terminal.

The Rapid Transit Act was signed into law in 1894 by New York Governor Roswell P. Flower, to authorize the subway's planning. John B. McDonald of the Rapid Transit Construction Company was awarded the contract for construction, William Barclay Parsons served as the city's chief engineer, and August Belmont II and his Interborough Rapid Transit Company financed the project. These fledgling subway lines, known as the IRT, were built in successive stages. Contract 1 broke ground in 1900 and opened in 1904, with its first line stretching the nine miles from City Hall to West 145th Street and Broadway. Contract 2 began construction in 1902, opening stations in Manhattan in 1905 and in Brooklyn in 1908.

The architects of these lines were Christopher Grant LaFarge (1862–1938) and George Lewis Heins (1860–1907), MIT graduates whose partnership had previously won the competition to design Manhattan's Cathedral Church of Saint John the Divine. They worked very well together—Heins specialized in structure, LaFarge in design and décor. Because of this arrangement, LaFarge took on the subway system's design elements, everything from mosaics to air vents. Heins, meanwhile, was appointed by New York Governor Theodore Roosevelt as State Architect to design Albany's governmental buildings. After the décor of the stations was completed, LaFarge moved on to other projects and was replaced by

Squire J. Vickers as the Public Service Commission's chief designing engineer and architect.

Under Vickers, the next phase of construction was known as the Dual Contracts (Contracts 3 and 4). These began in 1913, as the city worked with the IRT and the Brooklyn Rapid Transit Company (later known as the Brooklyn-Manhattan Transit Corporation) to simultaneously extend the IRT's system and build BMT lines. Subsequently, in June 1940, New York City took control over the subway systems and united them through the Independent City-Owned Subway System (IND), but these later stations are not included in this volume.

About the book:
The history of the New York subway system's décor is not widely chronicled. The primary sources for the captions in this book are Philip Coppola's *Silver Connections*, conversations with the artist, and additional online research. *Silver Connections* can be found at the New York Public Library and through New York Bound Books.

The illustrations are organized according to the order of station construction.

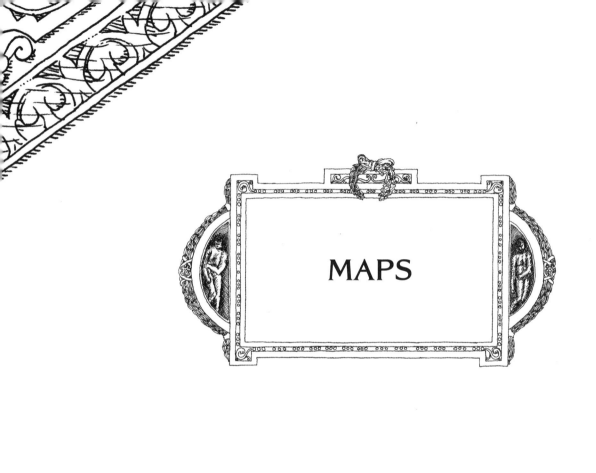

MAPS

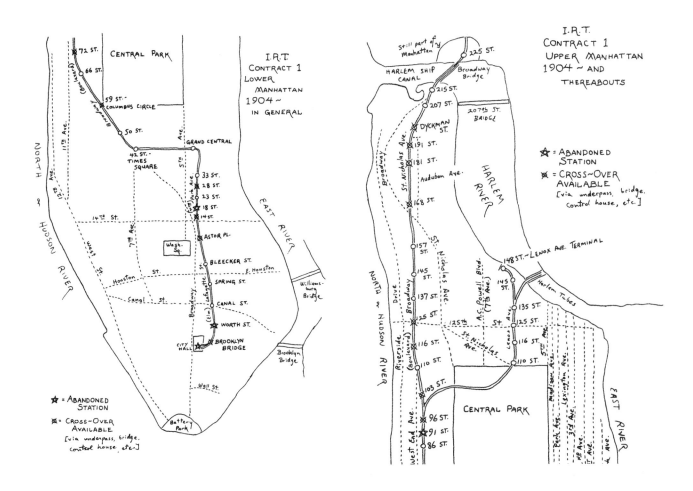

The I.R.T. Contract 1 in The Bronx ~ 1905

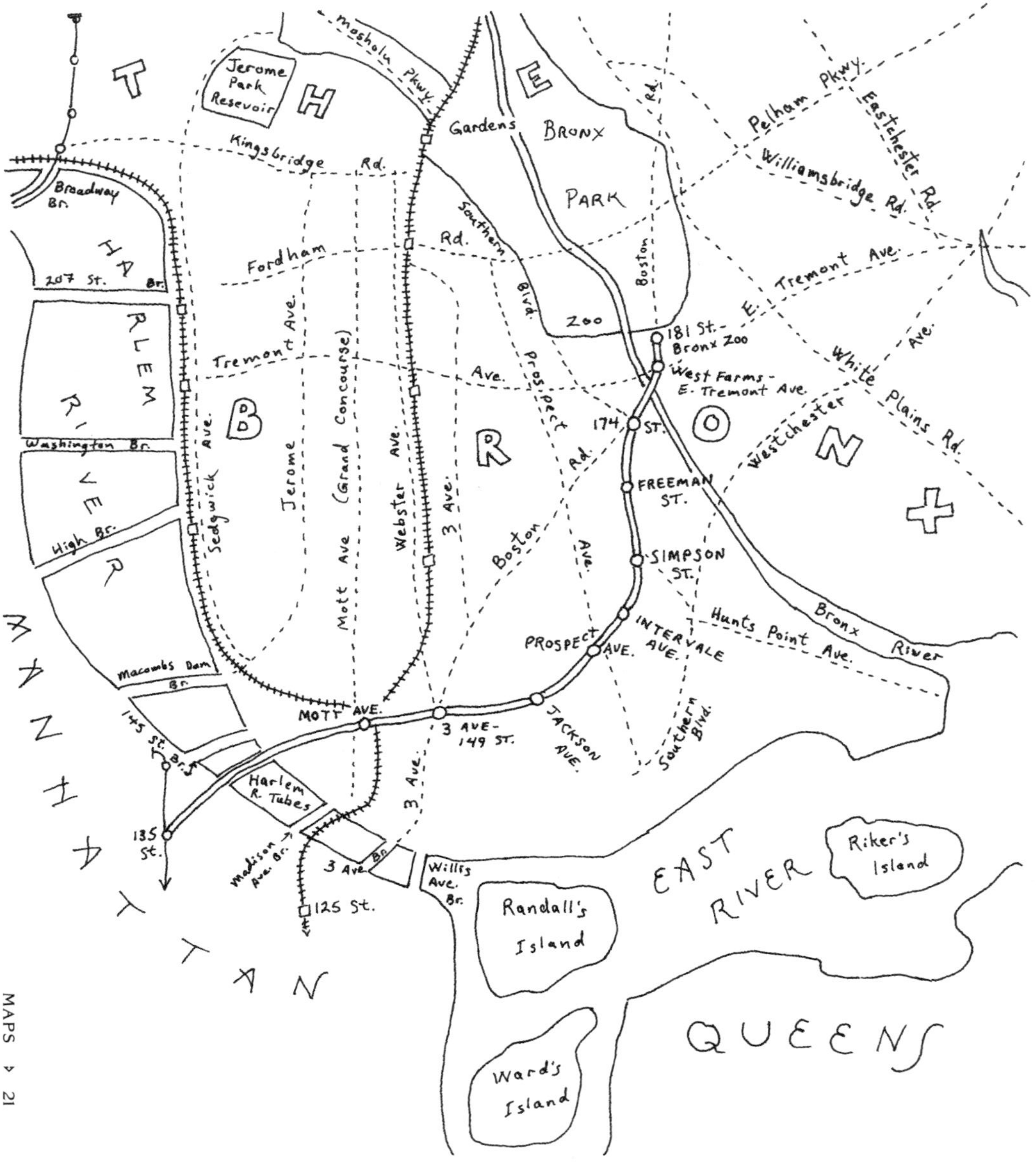

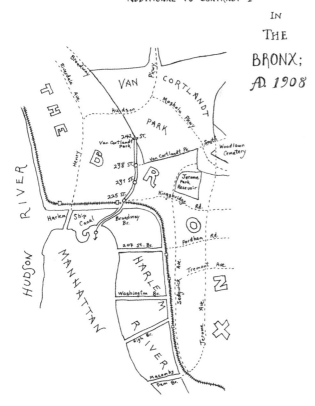

THE I.R.T. ~ THE VAN CORTLANDT PARK EXTENSION:
ADDITIONAL TO CONTRACT 1

IN
THE
BRONX;
A.D. 1908

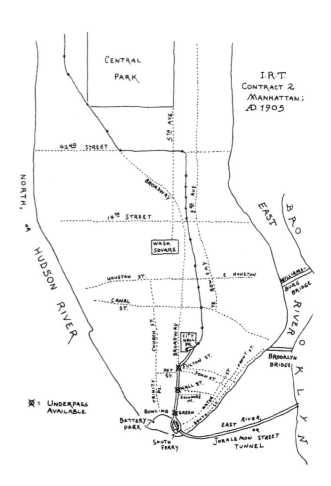

I.R.T.
CONTRACT 2
MANHATTAN;
A.D. 1905

⊠ = UNDERPASS
AVAILABLE

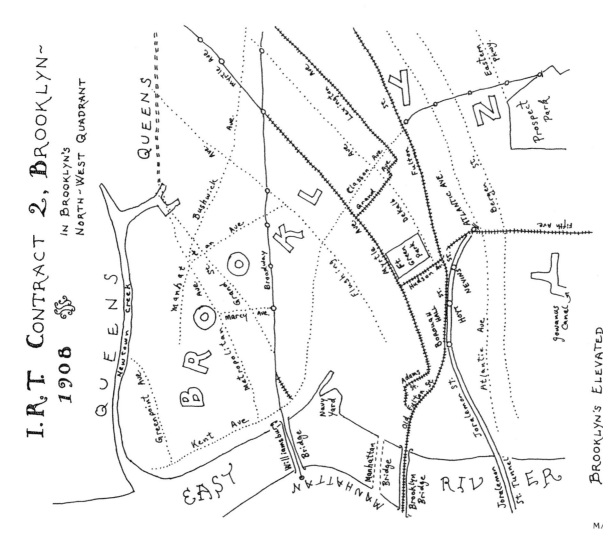

I.R.T. Contract 2, Brooklyn~

In Brooklyn's North-West Quadrant

1908

QUEENS

QUEENS

EAST RIVER

BROOKLYN

Newtown Creek

Greenpoint Ave.

Kent Ave.

Manhat Ave.

Grand St.

Metropolitan Ave.

Marcy Ave.

Broadway

Bushwick Ave.

Ave.

Ave.

Myrtle Ave.

Flush g

Lexington Ave.

Ave.

Grand Ave.

Classon Ave.

Myrtle Ave.

Fulton St.

Bergen St.

Eastern Pkwy

Prospect Park

ATLANTIC AVE.

Fifth Ave.

Gowanus Canal

Fulton St.

Ft. Green Park

Hudson Ave.

Borough Hall St.

NEVINS ST.

Hoyt

Adams St.

Old Fulton St.

Navy Yard

Williamsburg Bridge

Manhattan Bridge

Brooklyn Bridge

Atlantic Ave.

Joralemon St.

Joralemon St. Tunnel

MANHATTAN

Brooklyn's Elevated System: ●●●●●●●●●● ; as well as the Broadway, Franklin Av & Upper Myrtle Ave. lines (Present Transit)

MAPS ▷ 23

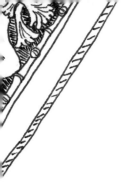

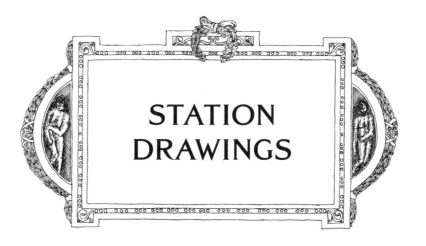

STATION
DRAWINGS

Brooklyn Bridge
Manhattan terminal
Structure demolished
(no longer visible)

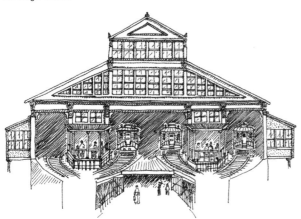

PARK ROW TERMINAL:
1900

LOOKING OUT FROM WITHIN PARK ROW TERMINAL: ca. 1887

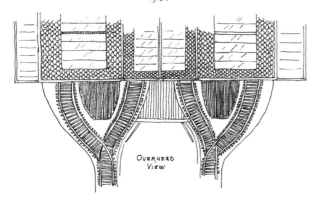

OVERHEAD
VIEW

INTERIOR OF PARK ROW TERMINAL ~ 1905

from The S.W. Stairway Landing: Wrought Iron & Cast

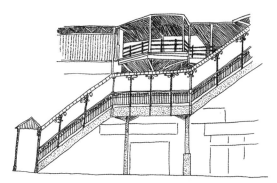

General View of S.W. Stairs: Along Franklin Ave.

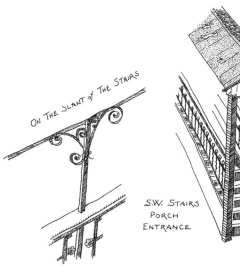

On The Slant of The Stairs

Outside View of Wrought Iron Rail

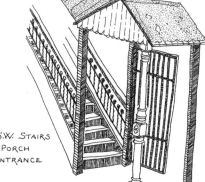

Prior To April, 1987

S.W. Stairs Porch Entrance

Franklin Avenue
Entrance stairway
Structure demolished
(no longer visible)

THE
PARK PLACE
STATION HOUSE:

INTERIOR VIEW

THREE
VARIETIES
of STAMPED
TIN

CEILING & WALL
DESIGNS

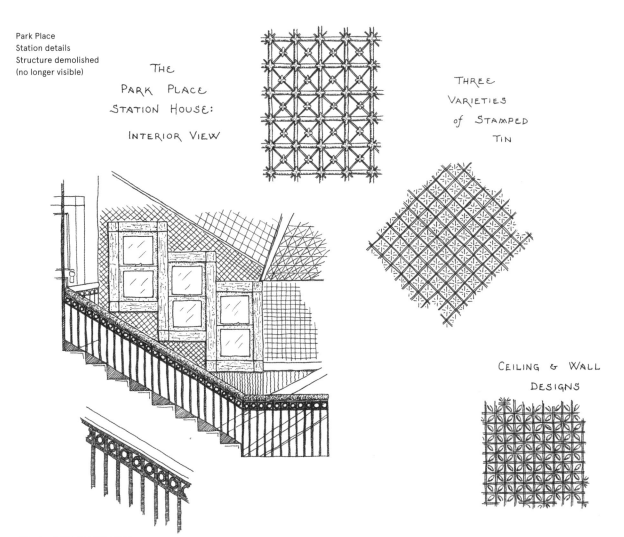

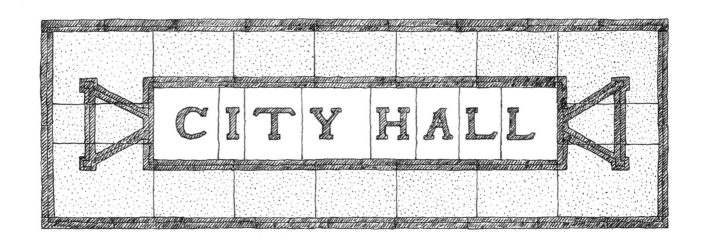

City Hall
Ceramic name panel
Closed station
(no longer visible)

City Hall
Mezzanine
Closed station
(no longer visible)

CITY HALL STATION

George Lewis Heins and Christopher Grant LaFarge envisioned the City Hall subway station as the crown jewel of the system. So when Chief Engineer William Barclay Parsons told them that the station itself would curve on a looped track, their thoughts raced ahead with visions of Romanesque arches. Heins and LaFarge would capitalize on this curvature, sending the walls vaulting overhead and filtering daylight in through three amethyst-hued, glass skylights. It was to be the quintessence of the subway's City Beautiful ideal.

This was one of the first stations LaFarge detailed, and he brought in the artisan Rafael Guastavino, who at the time was working with him on the Bronx Zoo animal houses, to build the arched tile ceiling and cast the name panels and the white and viridian tiles of the buttressing arches. When the station opened to the public on October 27, 1904, the press raved about its design, and more than fifteen thousand people were given passes for a ride.

As ridership rose and more cars were added, the longer trains could no longer navigate its tight loop and the station closed in 1946. Today this well-preserved station is occasionally opened for tours, and it remains a time capsule of all that the subway's creators had envisioned.

opposite:
City Hall
Platform
Closed station
(no longer visible)

right:
City Hall
Leaded glass skylight
Closed station
(no longer visible)

City Hall
Bronze
commemorative tablet
Closed station
(no longer visible)

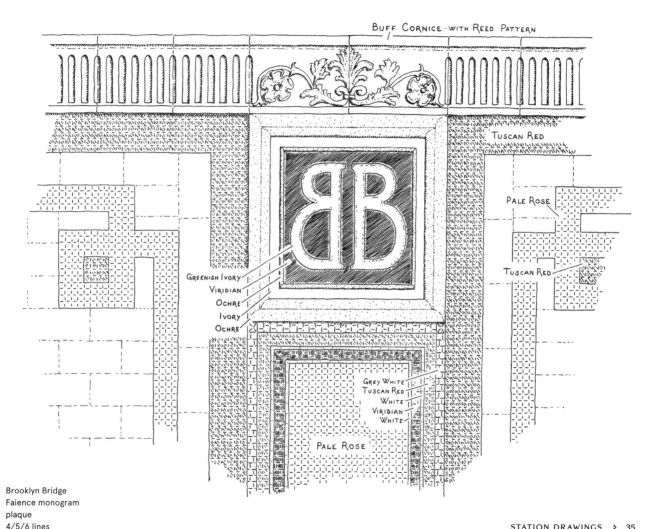

BUFF CORNICE · WITH REED PATTERN

TUSCAN RED

PALE ROSE

TUSCAN RED

GREENISH IVORY
VIRIDIAN
OCHRE
IVORY
OCHRE

GREY WHITE
TUSCAN RED
WHITE
VIRIDIAN
WHITE

PALE ROSE

Brooklyn Bridge
Faience monogram
plaque
4/5/6 lines

CANAL STREET MOSAIC NAME PANEL

Chief Engineer William Barclay Parsons came by one day with a message from the subway's financier, August Belmont II, ordering the architects to cut down on all the variety and create a standard design for the stations, because individualizing them was costing the banker a mint. So LaFarge worked on establishing a standard, repeatable design system for the stations and settled upon this mosaic format for name panels. While his design was standardized, these panels (and the station's design) are distinct in one specific way: it was a system Chief Engineer Parsons and his team formulated. How were the weary commuters, new to the very idea of subway travel, going to recognize their home station in an instant? The stations were color coded.

Felix Alcan, along with his dozen French and Italian craftsmen, hand cut and set the mosaics in 1904.

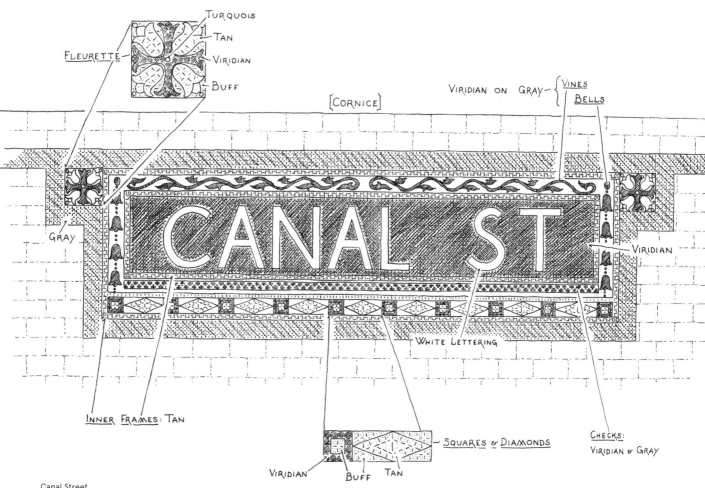

FLEURETTE
TURQUOIS
TAN
VIRIDIAN
BUFF

VIRIDIAN ON GRAY— { VINES, BELLS }

[CORNICE]

GRAY

CANAL ST

VIRIDIAN

WHITE LETTERING

INNER FRAMES: TAN

SQUARES & DIAMONDS

CHECKS: VIRIDIAN & GRAY

VIRIDIAN   BUFF   TAN

Canal Street
Mosaic name panel
6 line

Canal Street
Terracotta plaque
6 line

Bleecker Street
Faience name panel
6 line

BLEECKER STREET FAIENCE NAME PANEL

I n all the New York City subway system, you won't find any other name panels like these. This IRT station at Bleecker Street was one of the first to have its décor installed, and it benefitted from an early burst of LaFarge's enthusiasm to see the system live up to its City Beautiful aspirations. The faience name panel features enormous oval platters surrounded by a wide irregular frame of scrolls, blossoms, and acanthus clusters—all in a deep, lustrous cobalt blue. The station's eight original faience name panels survive to this day.

The panels were manufactured at Grueby Faience Company of South Boston, which was better known for its vases and the lamp bases it produced for Tiffany Studios.

MARBLE COPING

ROMAN   BRICK #59

opposite and right:
Bleecker Street
Faience name panel
and cornice
6 line

ASTOR PLACE FAIENCE BEAVER PLAQUE

Surely the Astor Place beaver plaque is the most fondly beheld of all the subway's iconic tableaux. Astor Place's namesake, John Jacob Astor, was one of the richest men in the world during his lifetime. Astor, labeled "the landlord of New York," made a great fortune in real estate. But other fortunes came before, most notably when he latched onto a fashionable trend of his time, when gentlemen of quality wore beaver-fur top hats. He entered into commerce with Native Americans and Canadian trappers, importing beaver pelts, and established his own trading post out in Oregon, which he modestly named Astoria. So it was beaver pelts that earned Astor his early fortune and enabled him to start buying up Manhattan piecemeal. Hence, the beaver plaques, to pay homage to his beginnings.

The plaques and cornice were fabricated by Grueby Faience, South Boston. Addison B. LeBoutillier probably guided the molding of these plaques.

Astor Place
Faience beaver plaque
6 line

IVORY

BROWN

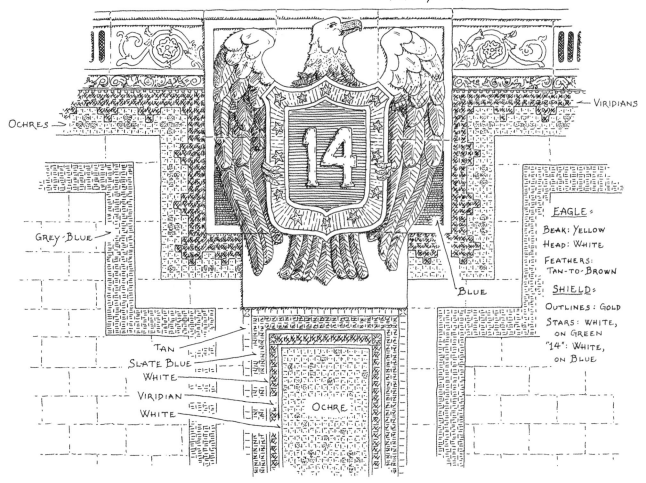

CORNICE & PLAQUE FRAME: LT. BROWN/OCHRE

VIRIDIANS

OCHRES

GREY-BLUE

BLUE

EAGLE:
BEAK: YELLOW
HEAD: WHITE
FEATHERS:
TAN-TO-BROWN

SHIELD:
OUTLINES: GOLD
STARS: WHITE,
ON GREEN
"14": WHITE,
ON BLUE

TAN
SLATE BLUE
WHITE
VIRIDIAN
WHITE

OCHRE

14TH STREET FAIENCE EAGLE PLAQUE

These eagle and escutcheon plaques adorn three stations on the first IRT line: Brooklyn Bridge, 14th Street / Union Square, and 33rd Street. So why are these magisterial eagles only at these three stations? If we associate these American bald eagles and their star-studded shields with American defense and strength, then armories are the answer. The 71st Regiment Armory stood just upstairs from the 33rd Street station, and the 42nd Infantry Armory was at Union Square. As for the eagles at Brooklyn Bridge, it's not readily known if there had been an armory there; unfortunately, these were covered up by a station reconstruction project in the 1960s.

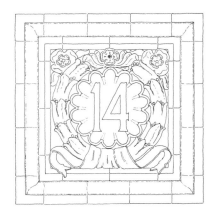

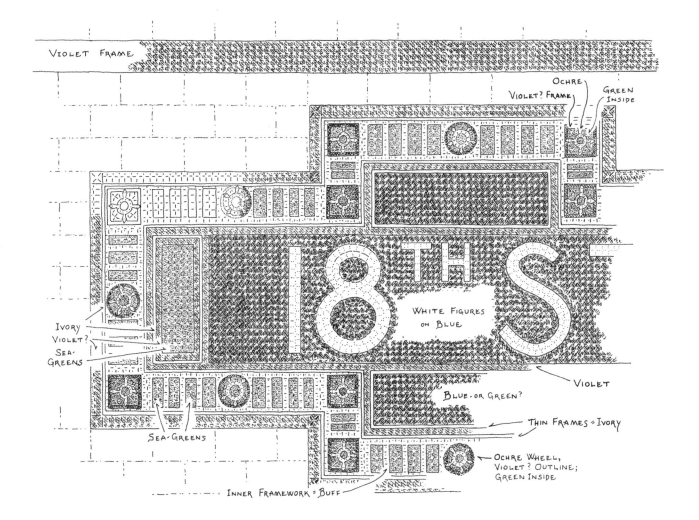

VIOLET FRAME

OCHRE
VIOLET? FRAME

GREEN
INSIDE

8 TH S

WHITE FIGURES
ON BLUE

IVORY
VIOLET?
SEA-
GREENS

VIOLET

BLUE - OR GREEN?

THIN FRAMES = IVORY

SEA-GREENS

OCHRE WHEEL,
VIOLET? OUTLINE;
GREEN INSIDE

INNER FRAMEWORK = BUFF

opposite:
18th Street
Mosaic name panel
6 line
Closed station
(no longer visible)

right:
18th Street
Faience plaque
6 line
Closed station
(no longer visible)

LT. GRAY   GRAY

NUMERALS:
 IVORY~GREEN

OVAL:
 VIRIDIAN

OVAL FRAME:
 WHITE

CARTOUCHE FRAME:
 OCHRE

BROWN

BROWNS

BUFFS

VERMILLION GLAZED MOSAIC BACKGROUND

GRAY GREEN

23RD ST

DARK VIRIDIAN

VIRIDIAN

BUFFS & BROWNS

TAN
BUFF
GRAY GREEN

BROWN

TAN

WHITE

23RD STREET MOSAIC NAME PANEL

The 23rd Street station was one of the first stations ready to have its artwork installed, so this sprawling mosaic name panel is one of LaFarge's earliest designs. There are no other name panels in the system like these, and sadly, it's now lost to history. In 1979 there were still two of the (possibly) eight name panels visible, but by the mid-1980s, the station had been renovated with beige wall tiles, obliterating the originals.

The mosaics were composed by Felix Alcan and his team of European craftsmen in 1903.

opposite:
23rd Street
Mosaic name panel
6 line
(no longer visible)

right:
23rd Street
Mosaic band
and faience cornice
6 line

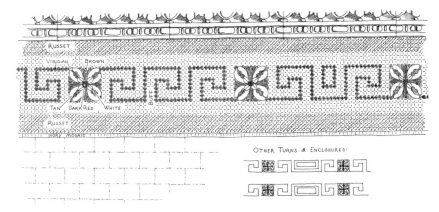

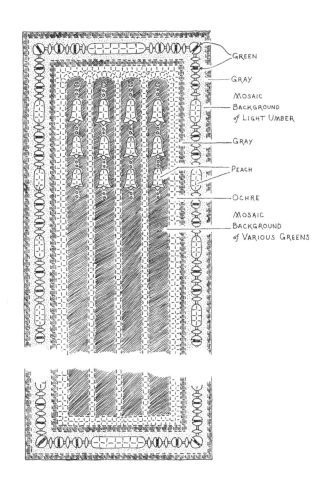

GREEN

GRAY

MOSAIC BACKGROUND of LIGHT UMBER

GRAY

PEACH

OCHRE

MOSAIC BACKGROUND of VARIOUS GREENS

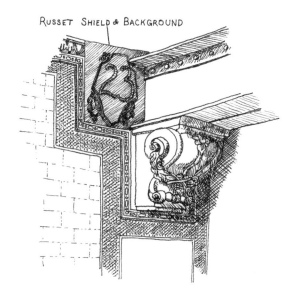

left:
23rd Street
Mosaic pilaster
6 line

right:
23rd Street
Faience corbel
6 line

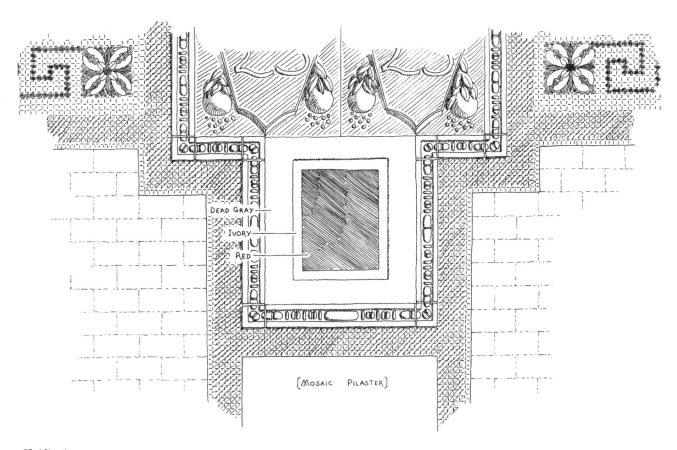

DEAD GRAY

IVORY

RED

[MOSAIC PILASTER]

23rd Street
Faience shields
and panel
6 line
(Shields no longer
visible)

28

TWENTY-EIGHTH
STREET

BLUE
OCHRE
PISTACHIO
TAN FRET IN BORDER
WHITE LETTERING

28th Street
Faience name panel
6 line

GRAY

TAN

EAGLE: BRONZE & WHITE

STARS: WHITE

NUMERALS: IVORY GREEN

SHIELD FRAMES: IVORY GREEN

BACKGROUND OF NUMERALS: DARK GREEN

BACKGROUND OF STARS: BLUE

VIRIDIAN

33rd Street
Faience eagle plaque
6 line

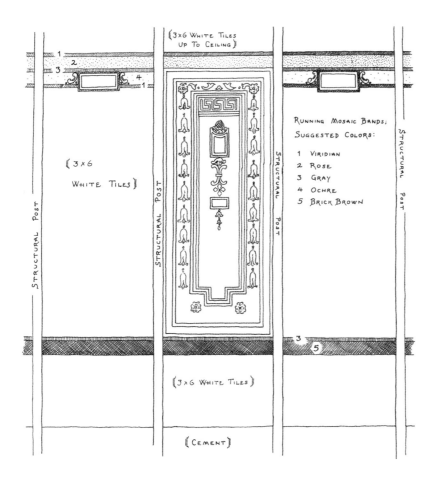

(3×6 WHITE TILES
UP TO CEILING)

(3 × 6
WHITE TILES)

(3 × 6 WHITE TILES)

(CEMENT)

RUNNING MOSAIC BANDS;
SUGGESTED COLORS:

1 VIRIDIAN
2 ROSE
3 GRAY
4 OCHRE
5 BRICK BROWN

STRUCTURAL POST
STRUCTURAL POST
STRUCTURAL POST
STRUCTURAL POST

42nd Street Shuttle
(Grand Central end)
Mosaic panel
S line
(no longer visible)

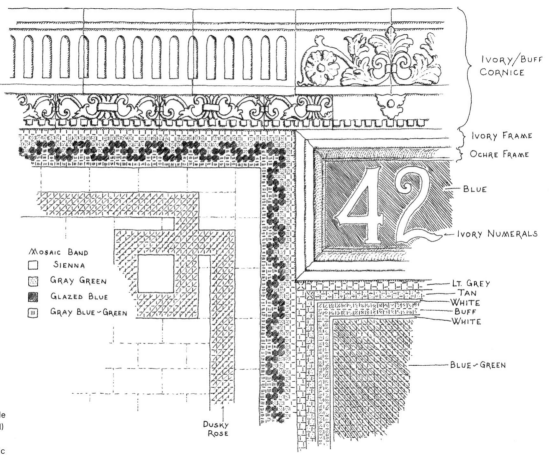

IVORY/BUFF
CORNICE

IVORY FRAME

OCHRE FRAME

BLUE

IVORY NUMERALS

LT. GREY
TAN
WHITE
BUFF
WHITE

BLUE-GREEN

MOSAIC BAND
☐ SIENNA
▨ GRAY GREEN
▦ GLAZED BLUE
⊞ GRAY BLUE-GREEN

DUSKY
ROSE

42nd Street Shuttle
(Times Square end)
Faience cornice
and plaque; mosaic
band and frame
S line
(no longer visible)

42nd Street Shuttle
(Times Square end)
Mosaic name panel
S line

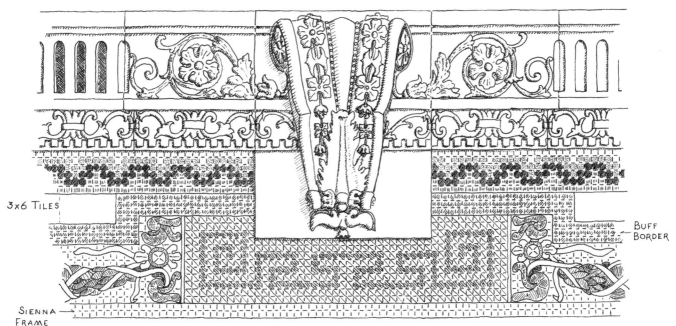

3×6 TILES

BUFF BORDER

SIENNA FRAME

["TIMES SQUARE" PLATE]

42nd Street Shuttle
(Times Square end)
Faience corbel
S line
(no longer visible)

COLUMBUS CIRCLE BEAM STRIPS

Few middle-class homes had their ceilings decorated with artistic moldings. That touch belonged to upper-class mansions, which had their own carriages and whose residents did not depend on subway travel. LaFarge wanted to bring that ornamentation to the commuter class, so along with cornices, paneling, and wainscots, there were decorative strips that ran along the ceiling beams, molded framework on the ceiling sections, and arabesque surrounds around light bulbs.

Though they appear to be plaster, these moldings are actually a three-dimensional wire construction built up with papier-mâché.

These ornamental moldings are the product of Charles Smithson and his team of craftsmen.

Columbus Circle
Beam strips and
ceiling frames
1 line

COLUMBUS CIRCLE

This was actually the very first station to receive its complete design from LaFarge's drawing board, and it is an example of his most lavish use of faience, featuring plaques of Christopher Columbus's *Santa Maria* and broad, modeled cornices. This extravagance was not lost on August Belmont II, the subway's financier, and he again pleaded to have the architecture simplified. His injunction led to a future reduction on faience and marble wainscots and increased reliance on mosaics and terracotta.

But for all its status, this station at 59th Street was neglectfully treated when, about thirty years after it opened, a new construction project demolished many of the plaques, cornices, and name panels.

Recently, the Metropolitan Transportation Authority (MTA) Office of Station Design reversed Columbus Circle's fortunes with a station facelift. The new design work is clad in terracotta, in homage to LaFarge's décor, with broad, flat, green cornices and plaques announcing "59" in large raised numerals. The new mosaic name panels, complete with ivy, bells, fleurettes, and other decorative designs, are faithful to the originals.

Original faience caravels were cast by Grueby Faience Company of South Boston in 1902.

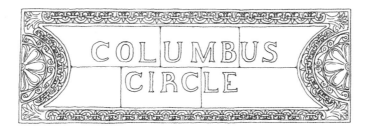

left:
Columbus Circle
Faience name panel
1 line
(no longer visible)

opposite:
Columbus Circle
Faience *Santa Maria*
plaque
1 line

VIRIDIAN & OLIVE

BUFF

PINK

PLAQUE:

SHIP & RIGGING:
LT. BROWN

SAILS & PENNANTS:
IVORY YELLOW

SKY:
DARK GREEN

SEA:
SEA GREEN

SEAGULLS:
IVORY YELLOW

LT. BROWN CORNICE

MEN

BUFF

opposite:
66th Street
Marble lintel
1 line
Former restroom
(no longer visible)

right:
72nd Street
Mosaic panel detail
1/2/3 lines

below:
72nd Street
Entrance house roofline
1/2/3 lines

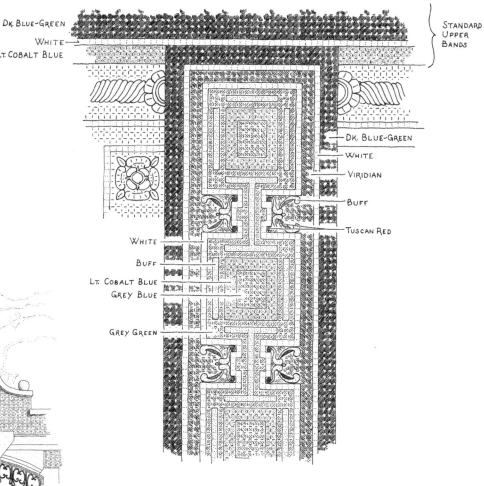

DK. BLUE-GREEN
WHITE
LT. COBALT BLUE

STANDARD UPPER BANDS

DK. BLUE-GREEN
WHITE
VIRIDIAN
BUFF
TUSCAN RED

WHITE
BUFF
LT. COBALT BLUE
GREY BLUE

GREY GREEN

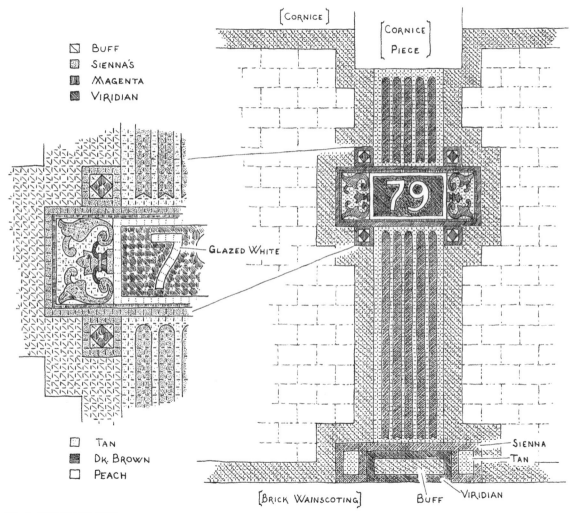

BUFF
SIENNA'S
MAGENTA
VIRIDIAN

[CORNICE]

[CORNICE PIECE]

GLAZED WHITE

79

TAN
DK. BROWN
PEACH

SIENNA
TAN

[BRICK WAINSCOTING]

BUFF   VIRIDIAN

opposite:
79th Street
Mosaic pilaster
1 line

right:
86th Street
Plaster ceiling frame
and light fixture
1 line

below:
86th Street
Faience cornice and
cornice plaque
1 line

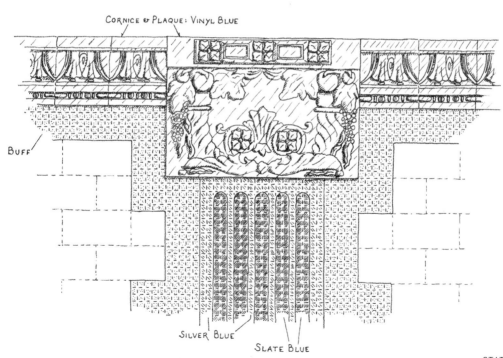

CORNICE & PLAQUE: VINYL BLUE

BUFF

SILVER BLUE

SLATE BLUE

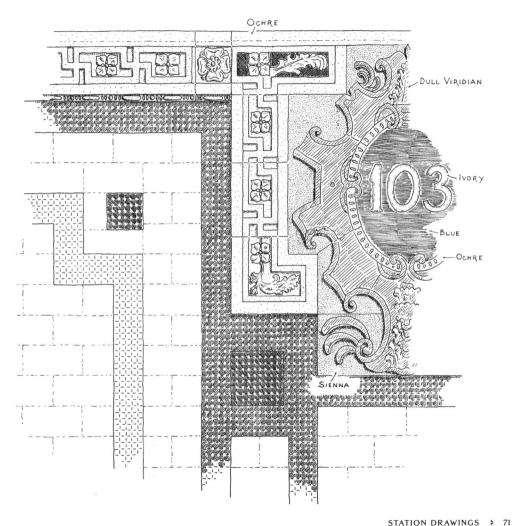

Ochre

Dull Viridian

Ivory

Blue

Ochre

Sienna

opposite:
96th Street
Faience plaque and
mosaic frameworks
1/2/3 lines
(mosaic frameworks
no longer visible)

right:
103rd Street
Faience plaque and
mosaic frameworks
1 line

DARK VIRIDIAN

BUFF

Cathedral Parkway /
110th Street
Faience plaque and
mosaic frameworks
1 line

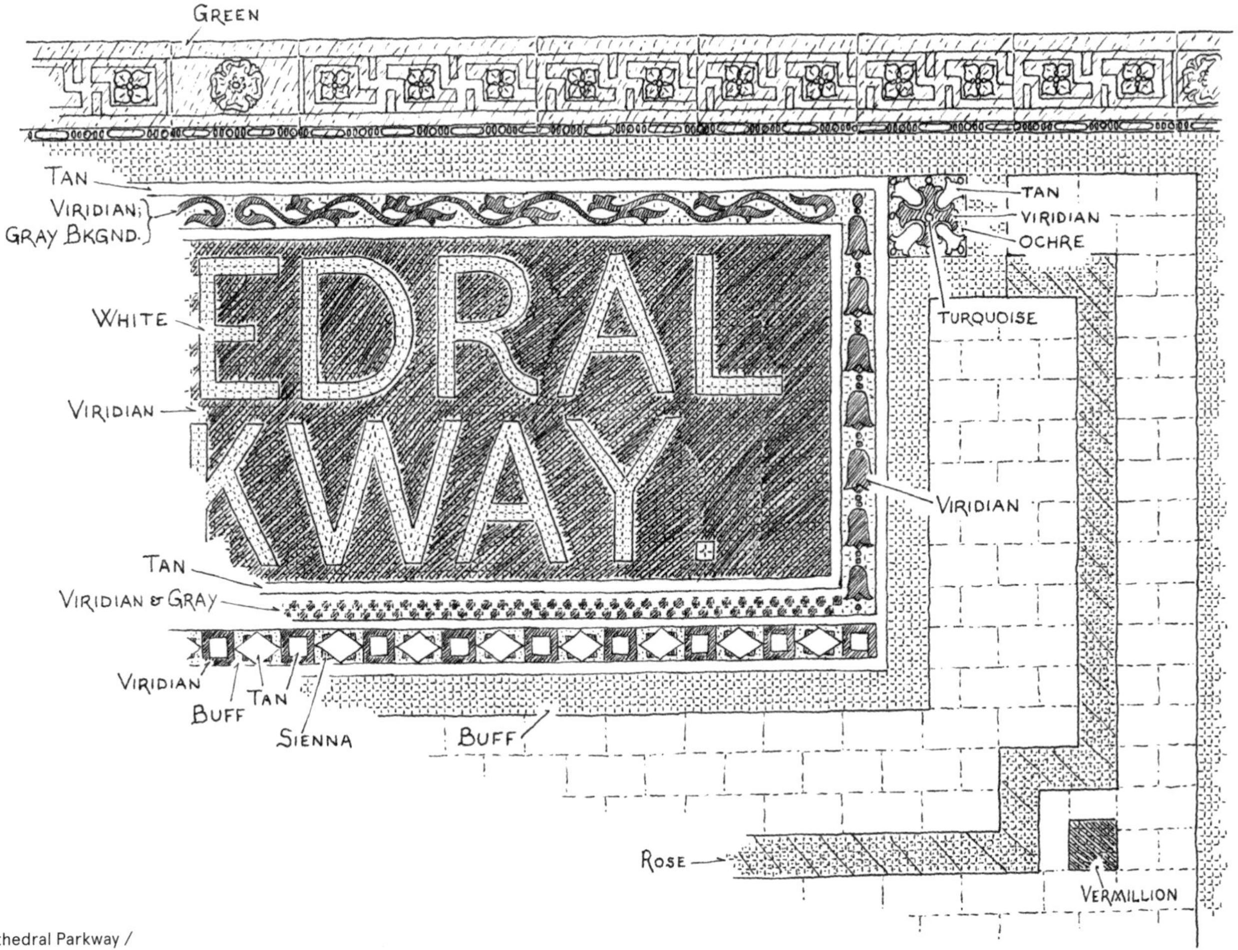

GREEN

TAN
VIRIDIAN;
GRAY BKGND.

TAN
VIRIDIAN
OCHRE

WHITE

TURQUOISE

VIRIDIAN

VIRIDIAN

TAN
VIRIDIAN & GRAY

VIRIDIAN
BUFF TAN
SIENNA

BUFF

ROSE

VERMILLION

Cathedral Parkway /
110th Street
Mosaic name panel
1 line

COLUMBIA UNIVERSITY SEAL PLAQUE

Columbia University established its uptown campus through the 1890s, about ten years before the IRT arrived at 116th Street. The wall plaque is a rendition of the university's seal—the grand lady, in the center, is the university, and the three cherubs represent the student body. The seal itself was designed by the Reverend Dr. Samuel Johnson, the first President of Kings College, whose original campus was down at Chambers Street in pre-Revolutionary New York. Kings College then changed its name to the present "Columbia" after the American Revolution.

This is one of the more beautiful Contract 1 stations, and its lavishness may have had something to do with the fact that the subway's chief engineer, William Barclay Parsons, graduated from Columbia's School of Mines in 1882.

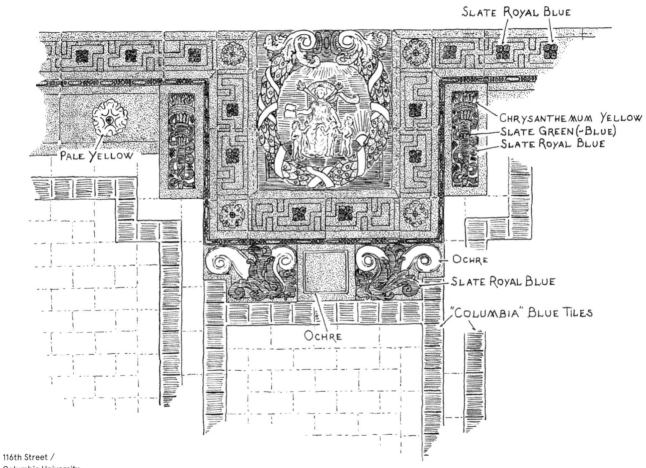

SLATE ROYAL BLUE

CHRYSANTHEMUM YELLOW
SLATE GREEN (~BLUE)
SLATE ROYAL BLUE

PALE YELLOW

OCHRE

SLATE ROYAL BLUE

"COLUMBIA" BLUE TILES

OCHRE

116th Street /
Columbia University
seal plaque
1 line

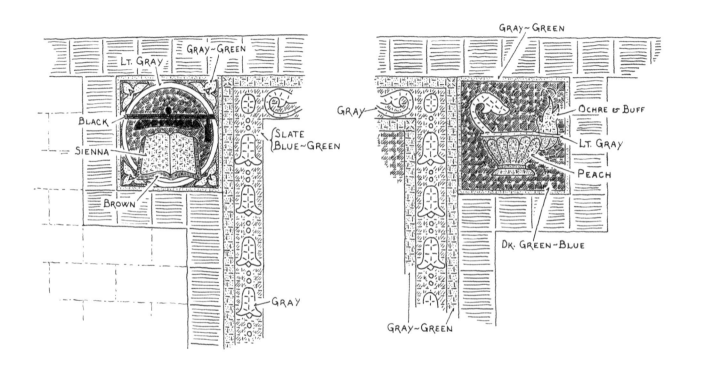

LT. GRAY

GRAY~GREEN

BLACK

SIENNA

BROWN

SLATE
BLUE~GREEN

GRAY

GRAY~GREEN

GRAY

GRAY~GREEN

OCHRE & BUFF

LT. GRAY

PEACH

DK. GREEN~BLUE

116th Street /
Columbia University
Mosaic name panel
details
1 line

116th Street /
Columbia University
Pilaster beam strip
1 line

OLIVE-GREEN BAND

137TH STREET
CITY COLLEG

BELLS:
  BROWN KNOBS
  LT. & DK. GREEN BODY

FLEURETTES:
  OCHRE CENTER
  BROWN CROSS
  LT. & DK. GREEN LEAVES

137th Street /
City College
Mosaic name panel
1 line

137TH STREET MOSAIC NAME PANEL

It is likely that the first version of this stop's decoration, dating to 1904, had standard mosaic name tablets and the panel "137th Street" in white on blue. But City College wanted its existence acknowledged in the station in the same way that Columbia University was named two stations to the south. City College filed their first petition with the Rapid Transit Commission within a year of the subway's début, but its request was declined. City College tried again and again over the next decade until the Public Service Commission agreed to install modest placards announcing "City College"

on the station's walls. Not satisfied with such a token response, the college resumed its efforts and by 1920 the Transit Construction Commission agreed to a name change, though it demanded that the college fund the project itself. The college's subsequent fund drive was so successful that 137th Street benefitted with the installation of twelve beautiful mosaic panels, resplendent in the lavender and black colors of the college. Two of these panels are still visible.

The identities of the designer and artisans are unknown.

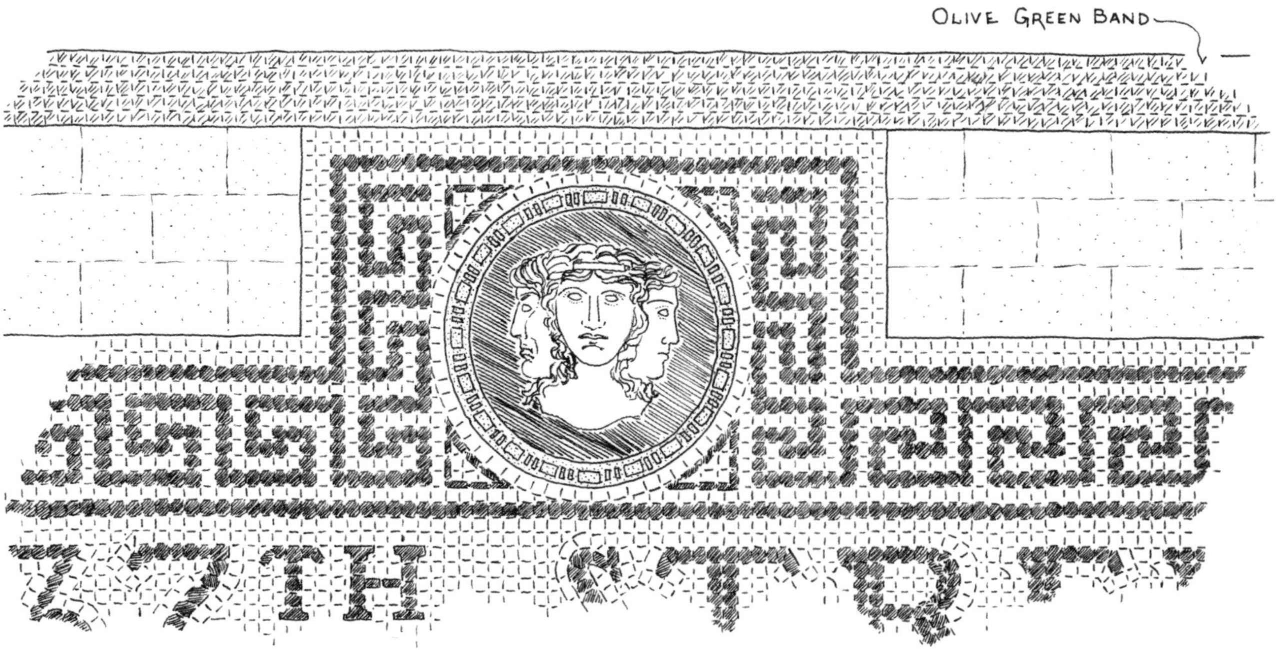

OLIVE GREEN BAND

137th Street /
City College
Terracotta medallion
and mosaic
name panel detail
1 line

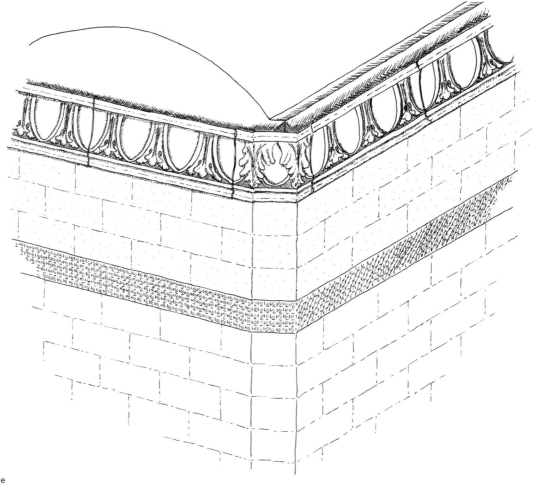

137th Street /
City College
Terracotta cornice
1 line
(no longer visible)

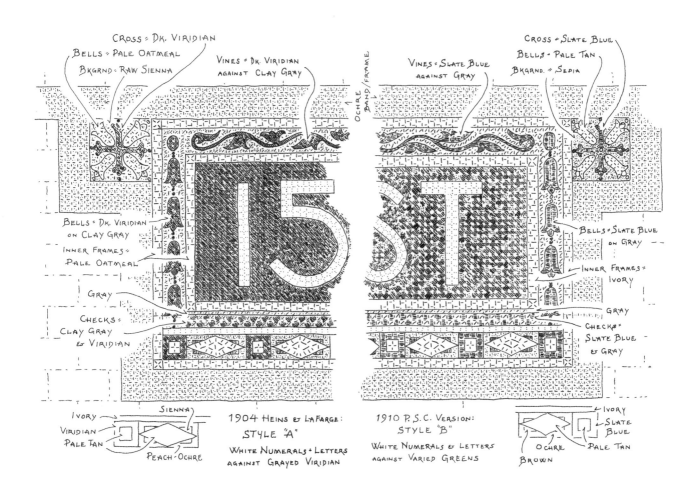

CROSS = DK. VIRIDIAN
BELLS = PALE OATMEAL
BKGRND = RAW SIENNA

VINES = DK. VIRIDIAN
AGAINST CLAY GRAY

OCHRE BAND/FRAME

VINES = SLATE BLUE
AGAINST GRAY

CROSS = SLATE BLUE
BELLS = PALE TAN
BKGRND = SEPIA

BELLS = DK. VIRIDIAN
ON CLAY GRAY

INNER FRAMES =
PALE OATMEAL

GRAY

CHECKS =
CLAY GRAY
& VIRIDIAN

BELLS = SLATE BLUE
ON GRAY

INNER FRAMES =
IVORY

GRAY

CHECKS =
SLATE BLUE
& GRAY

IVORY
VIRIDIAN
PALE TAN

SIENNA

PEACH-OCHRE

1904 HEINS & LAFARGE:
STYLE "A"
WHITE NUMERALS & LETTERS
AGAINST GRAYED VIRIDIAN

1910 P.S.C. VERSION:
STYLE "B"
WHITE NUMERALS & LETTERS
AGAINST VARIED GREENS

IVORY
SLATE
BLUE
PALE TAN

OCHRE
BROWN

opposite:
157th Street
Mosaic name panels
1 line

right:
168th Street
Mosaic edging
1 line

below:
145th Street
Terracotta plaque
and cornice
1 line

MOSAIC BORDER TO OLD ELEVATOR AREA [FLATTENED OUT]

GRAY-BLUE

168TH STREET BRIDGE LEADING
TO 1906 ELEVATOR ALCOVE

This is almost like needlepoint rendered in mosaic. This ribband of triangles and fleurettes surrounds a stone ceiling-wreath that once bore a light fixture above the overpass bridge leading to the original 1906 elevator bank. The ceiling mosaics were corrupted by water pressure and fallen out in some places, but recently LaFarge's delicate pattern has been reproduced to look like the original. The elevators have been removed completely. Another piece of the city's subway has passed into history.

The mosaics were composed by Felix Alcan and his European craftsmen in 1904.

168th Street
Bridge leading to
1906 elevator alcove
1 line
Elevators removed

VARIOUS FLEURETTES AT 168ᵀᴴ ST.:
* * * *
ON ORIGINAL PLATFORMS;
SEE ILLUS. # 77
* * * *
UPTOWN SIDE EXT. BAND;

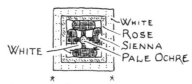

WHITE
ROSE
SIENNA
PALE OCHRE
WHITE

* *
UPTOWN SIDE EXT. PILASTER;
SEE THIS ILLUS.
* *
UPTOWN SIDE EXT. PIER;
• SEE ILLUS. # 73

* * * *

DOWNTOWN SIDE EXT. BAND;

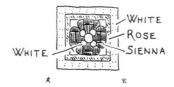

WHITE
ROSE
SIENNA
WHITE

* *

DOWNTOWN SIDE EXT. PILASTER
& (IN SMALLER VERSION) PIER;

WHITE
ROSE
SIENNA
WHITE

left and opposite:
168th Street
Mosaic pilaster and
fleurettes
1 line

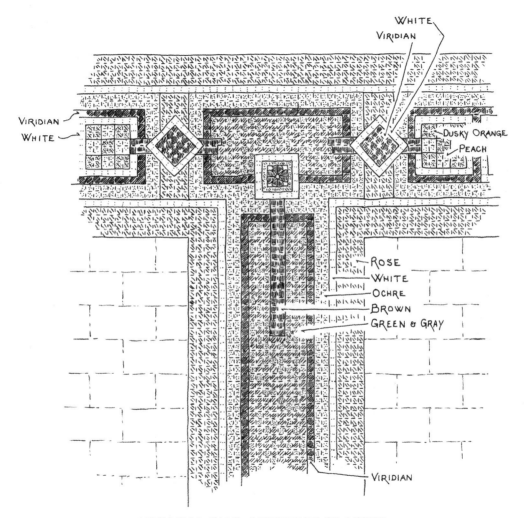

WHITE
VIRIDIAN

VIRIDIAN
WHITE

DUSKY ORANGE
PEACH

ROSE
WHITE
OCHRE
BROWN
GREEN & GRAY

VIRIDIAN

UPTOWN SIDE EXTENSION PILASTER

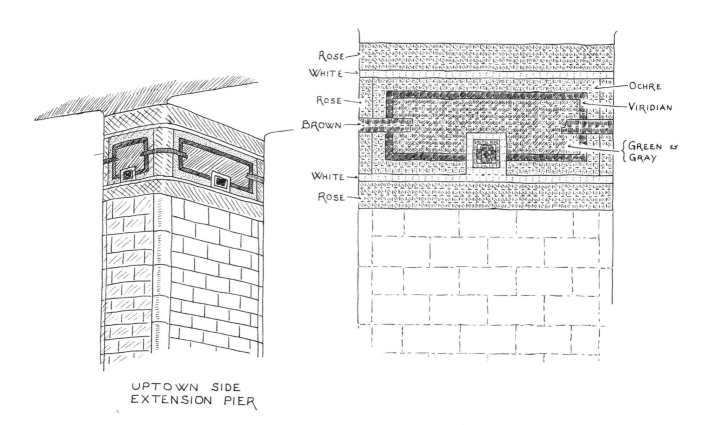

ROSE
WHITE
ROSE
BROWN
WHITE
ROSE

OCHRE
VIRIDIAN
GREEN & GRAY

UPTOWN SIDE
EXTENSION PIER

168th Street
Mosaic bands
1 line

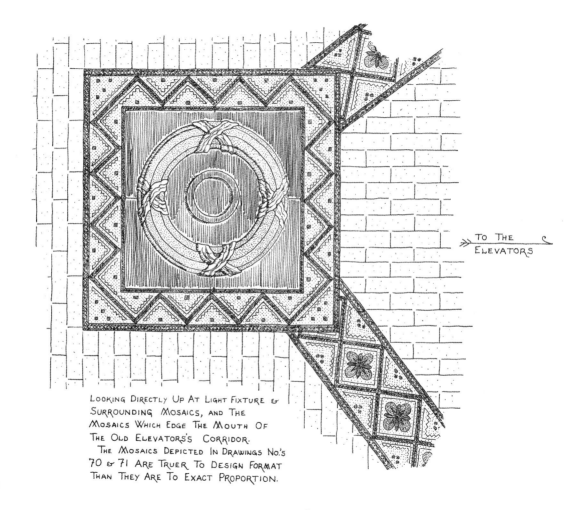

TO THE
ELEVATORS

LOOKING DIRECTLY UP AT LIGHT FIXTURE &
SURROUNDING MOSAICS, AND THE
MOSAICS WHICH EDGE THE MOUTH OF
THE OLD ELEVATORS'S CORRIDOR.
THE MOSAICS DEPICTED IN DRAWINGS No.'s
70 & 71 ARE TRUER TO DESIGN FORMAT
THAN THEY ARE TO EXACT PROPORTION.

168th Street
Faience ceiling wreath
and mosaic border
1 line
Rebuilt with new frame

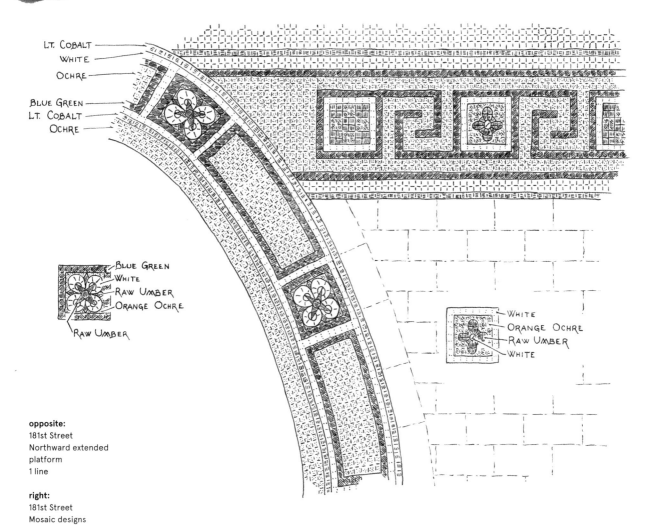

LT. COBALT
WHITE
OCHRE

BLUE GREEN
LT. COBALT
OCHRE

BLUE GREEN
WHITE
RAW UMBER
ORANGE OCHRE

RAW UMBER

WHITE
ORANGE OCHRE
RAW UMBER
WHITE

opposite:
181st Street
Northward extended
platform
1 line

right:
181st Street
Mosaic designs
1 line

181ST STREET ROSETTE

Deep under the hills of Washington Heights, 126 feet below ground, lies the 181st Street station. There is an oversize rosette crowning the name panels, and everything seems done on a grand scale. The large mosaic band of frets and fleurettes arches with the barrel vault just as it begins to curve over the heads of the commuters. Form was function, and all of the architectural arrangements—plaques, cornices, paneling, floral designs on the walls, even the lowly air vents—were meant to remind the commuters of a pleasant room, providing comfort to city folk unaccustomed to riding a train under the earth. (181st Street station is actually not the deepest station in the system. That distinction goes to the 191st Street station, built in 1911, which runs 180 feet below ground.)

The mosaics were composed by Felix Alcan and his European craftsmen in 1904.

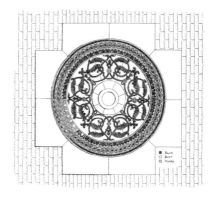

181st Street
Ceiling wreath
1 line

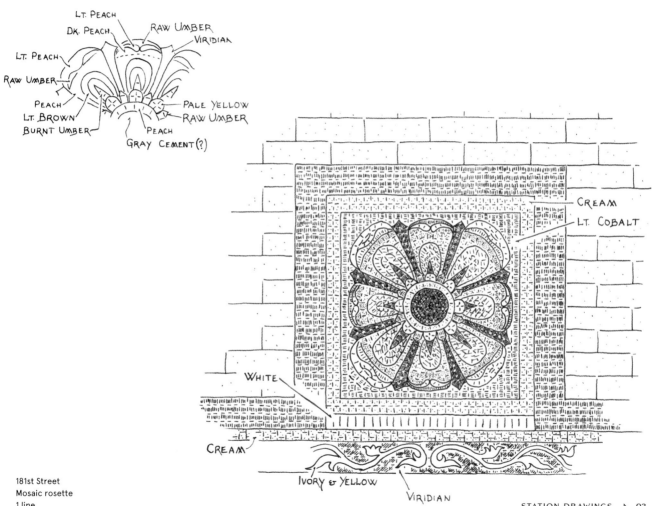

LT. PEACH
DK. PEACH
RAW UMBER
VIRIDIAN
LT. PEACH
RAW UMBER
PEACH
LT. BROWN
BURNT UMBER
PALE YELLOW
RAW UMBER
PEACH
GRAY CEMENT (?)

CREAM
LT. COBALT

WHITE

CREAM

IVORY & YELLOW
VIRIDIAN

181st Street
Mosaic rosette
1 line

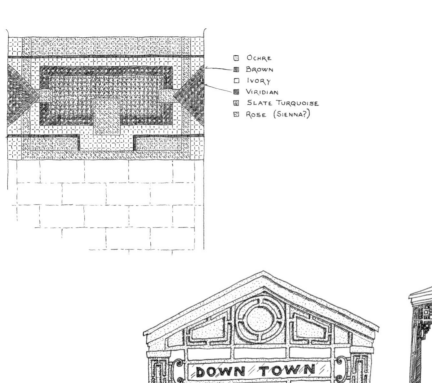

left:
191st Street
Mosaic band
1 line

below:
215th Street
Stairway porch
1 line

☐ OCHRE
▦ BROWN
☐ IVORY
▩ VIRIDIAN
▧ SLATE TURQUOISE
▨ ROSE (SIENNA?)

DOWN TOWN

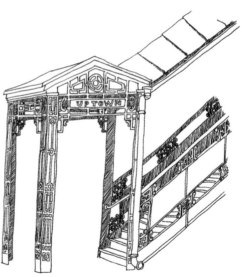

UP TOWN

110th Street /
Central Park North
Mosaic panel detail
2/3 lines

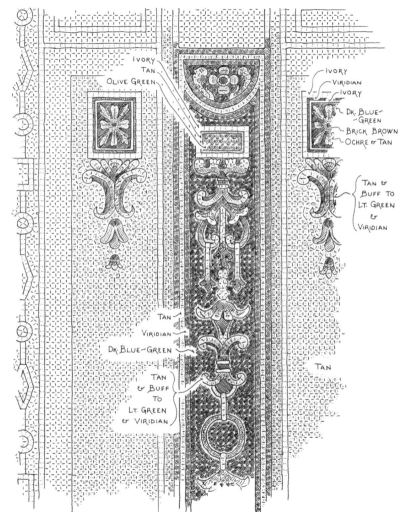

IVORY
TAN
OLIVE GREEN

IVORY
VIRIDIAN
IVORY
DK. BLUE-
GREEN
BRICK BROWN
OCHRE & TAN

TAN &
BUFF TO
LT. GREEN
&
VIRIDIAN

TAN
VIRIDIAN
DK. BLUE-GREEN

TAN
& BUFF
TO
LT. GREEN
& VIRIDIAN

TAN

110TH STREET AND LENOX MOSAIC PANEL

This is just one detail of the magnificent tapestry panels tucked away in the 110th Street and Lenox Avenue station. A strand of mosaic jewels runs around a wide border, framing a chain of floral horns and caps, jacquard straps, and jade rings descending through the central panel, flanked by boxed fleurettes and verdant curls. LaFarge created four distinct design formats for these "oriental rug" panels, which graced four stations of the early IRT lines in Manhattan. Aside from this station, there is one other station whose panels are still visible: 72nd Street and Broadway. The Bowling Green station's were lost in 1977, and the Grand Central panels were destroyed in a fire in 1964.

The mosaics were composed by Felix Alcan and his European craftsmen in 1904.

opposite:
110th Street / Central
Park North
Mosaic panel detail
2/3 lines

125TH STREET TERRACOTTA PLAQUE AND CORNICE

The basic design of this "125" cartouche plaque is a recurring décor element featured in a good quarter of the earliest stations. LaFarge initially wanted the subway's plaques and cornices fashioned in faience, but in many instances, as costs mounted, the later stations needed to be trimmed, as this one is, in the less costly terracotta. LaFarge's decorative wall of white tiles, mosaics, and ceramics is actually a shell, approximately a half-foot thick, standing about two inches away from the rough structural wall. This was a deliberate strategy of the station's construction. Through holes in the cornice, air may flow between the structural and the finish walls of these stations. The engineers intended, by this device, to eliminate the destructive effects underground water pressure could have on these subterranean walls, hopefully keeping everything dry within.

Plaque and cornice were cast by Atlantic Terra Cotta Works, Staten Island, New York, in 1904; it's possible that they were modeled by William D. Frerichs.

125th Street
Terracotta plaque
and cornice
2/3 lines

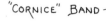
"CORNICE" BAND

- ☐ WHITE
- ☐ TAN
- ☒ BLUE
- ☐ OCHRE

145th Street
Mosaic rendition of
terracotta plaque
2/3 lines

145TH STREET MOSAIC NAME PANEL

In 1904 this station was the end of the line. (The only facility farther north was a train storage yard at 148th Street.) The tulip frieze cornice and cartouche number plaques here were originally made of terracotta, but within a few years of the station's public debut, a section of the wall was altered and rebuilt with mosaic renditions of the terracotta plaques.

This mosaic plaque is likely by Felix Alcan and his European craftsmen.

"CORNICE": TAN MOSAIC

P. S. C. NAME PANEL

VINES + BELLS:
BLUE, ON GRAY-BLUE

IRON GRAY

IVORY

WHITE

GREEN

FLEURETTE:
- CROSS = BLUE
  BELLS = IVORY
- BACKGROUND =
  GOLDEN SIENNA
- CENTER DOT
  IN CROSS =
  GOLDEN SIENNA

BLUE + GRAY-BLUE

IVORY

BLUE   BUFF   BROWN

135TH

opposite:
135th Street
Mosaic name panel
2/3 lines

below:
149th Street /
Grand Concourse
Mosaic band
2/5 lines

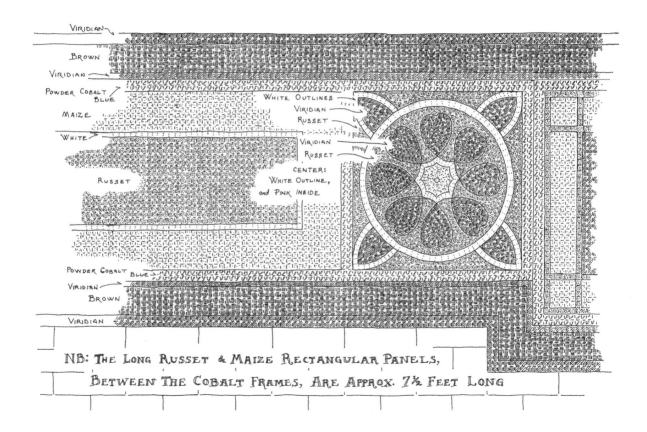

VIRIDIAN
BROWN
VIRIDIAN
POWDER COBALT BLUE
MAIZE
WHITE
RUSSET
POWDER COBALT BLUE
VIRIDIAN
BROWN
VIRIDIAN

WHITE OUTLINES
VIRIDIAN
RUSSET
VIRIDIAN
RUSSET
CENTER:
WHITE OUTLINE,
and PINK INSIDE

NB: THE LONG RUSSET & MAIZE RECTANGULAR PANELS,
BETWEEN THE COBALT FRAMES, ARE APPROX. 7½ FEET LONG

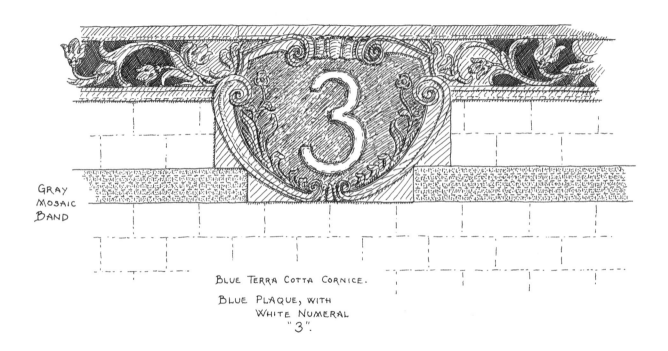

GRAY
MOSAIC
BAND

BLUE TERRA COTTA CORNICE.

BLUE PLAQUE, WITH
WHITE NUMERAL
"3".

3rd Avenue
Terracotta plaque
2/5 lines
(no longer visible)

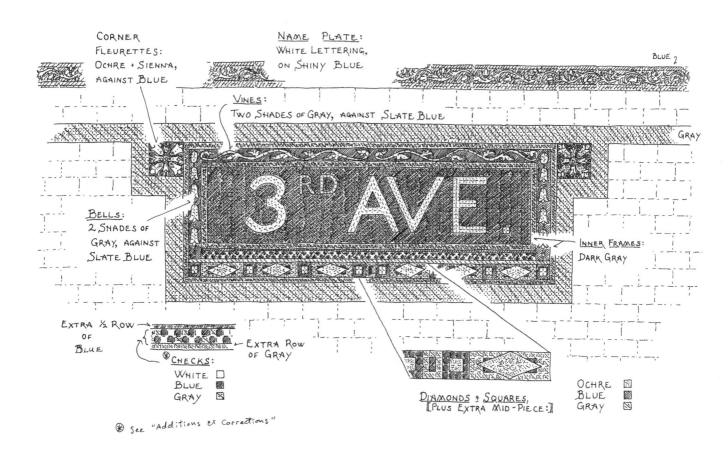

CORNER
FLEURETTES:
OCHRE + SIENNA,
AGAINST BLUE

NAME PLATE:
WHITE LETTERING,
ON SHINY BLUE

BLUE 2

VINES:
TWO SHADES OF GRAY, AGAINST SLATE BLUE

GRAY

3RD AVE.

BELLS:
2 SHADES OF
GRAY, AGAINST
SLATE BLUE

INNER FRAMES:
DARK GRAY

EXTRA ½ ROW
OF
BLUE

EXTRA ROW
OF GRAY

CHECKS:
WHITE ☐
BLUE ▨
GRAY ▨

DIAMONDS & SQUARES,
[PLUS EXTRA MID-PIECE:]

OCHRE ▨
BLUE ▨
GRAY ▨

⊛ SEE "Additions & Corrections"

3rd Avenue
Mosaic name panel
2/5 lines
(no longer visible)

FULTON STREET STEAMBOAT
FAIENCE PLAQUE

When Robert Fulton first brought the steamboat to New York in 1807, it was nicknamed "Fulton's Folly," for nobody believed a "steam engine" could possibly have the strength to turn a heavy paddle wheel and propel a vessel upstream. But Fulton knew better. He'd already run a steamboat in Paris in 1803, where he found a wealthy New York benefactor, Robert Livingston. Later, with Livingston's backing, Fulton steamed up the Hudson from the Battery to Albany and back, nearly halving the time it took a sailboat to make the same trip.

Four of these faience plaques survive on the west side of the station, but the east side platform, along with its faience plaques, was entirely bricked over in the 1980s.

These faience plaques were fabricated by Rookwood Faience, Cincinnati, Ohio, in 1905. It is possible the master mold was modeled by John Dee Wareham.

NARROW FRAMES:
   IVORY
FESTOONS & HANGING BOUQUETS:
   OCHRE, WITH IVORY RIBANDS
FULTON STEAMBOAT PLAQUE:
   SKY: LT. BLUE & COBALT
   LAND: PALE GREEN HILLS. GREEN TREES & SHRUBS
   SHORE: OCHRE, WITH BLUE WATERLINE
   WATER: PALE BLUE & WHITE
   BOAT: BLUE STACK & HULL, WHITE GUNWALE,
      OCHRE SIDEWHEEL & "SPEAR"(?)
   FLAG: RED, WHITE, & BLUE
   SMOKE: MED. DK. BLUE - TO - BROWN~GRAY
   MEN IN BOAT: BLUE

Color scheme
Fulton Street
Faience plaque
4/5 lines

Fulton Street
Faience plaque
4/5 lines

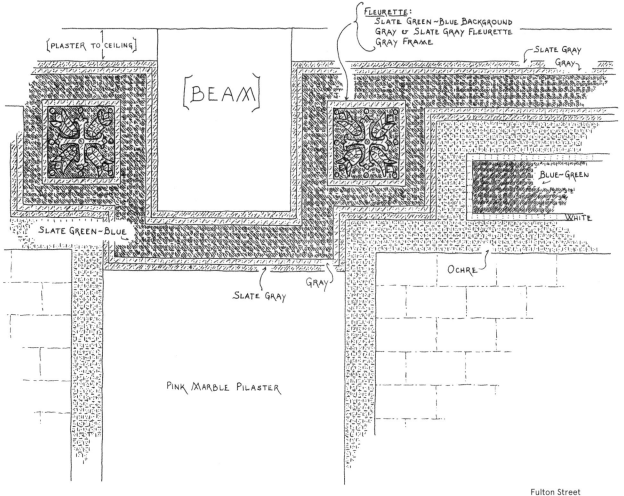

[PLASTER TO CEILING]

[BEAM]

FLEURETTE:
SLATE GREEN~BLUE BACKGROUND
GRAY & SLATE GRAY FLEURETTE
GRAY FRAME

SLATE GRAY
GRAY

BLUE~GREEN

WHITE

SLATE GREEN~BLUE

SLATE GRAY

GRAY

OCHRE

PINK MARBLE PILASTER

Fulton Street
Mosaic designs
4/5 lines

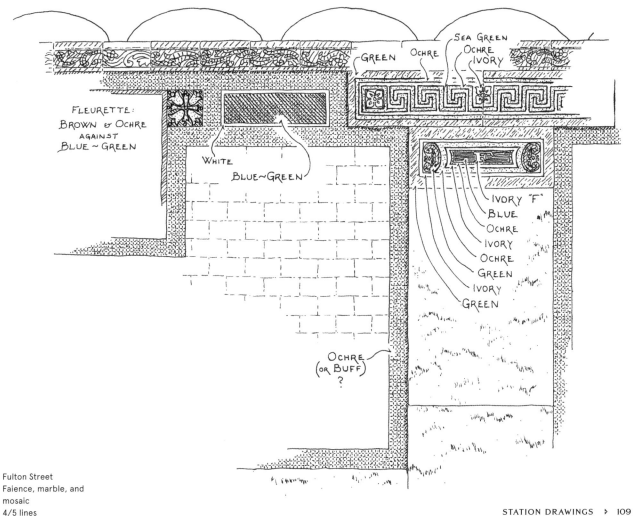

FLEURETTE:
BROWN & OCHRE
AGAINST
BLUE ~ GREEN

WHITE
BLUE~GREEN

GREEN   OCHRE   SEA GREEN
OCHRE
IVORY

IVORY "F"
BLUE
OCHRE
IVORY
OCHRE
GREEN
IVORY
GREEN

OCHRE
(OR BUFF)
?

Fulton Street
Faience, marble, and
mosaic
4/5 lines

Fulton Street
Mosaic name panel
4/5 lines

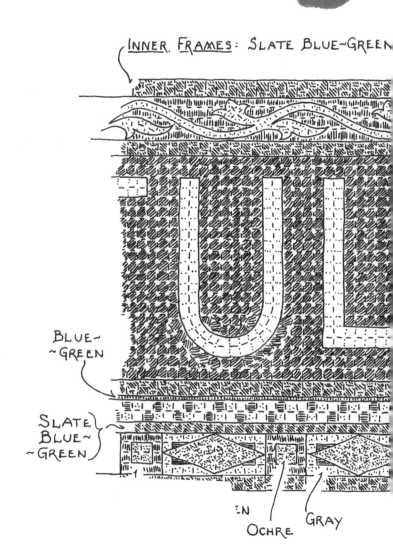

INNER FRAMES: SLATE BLUE~GREEN

BLUE~
~GREEN

SLATE
BLUE~
~GREEN

IN
OCHRE

GRAY

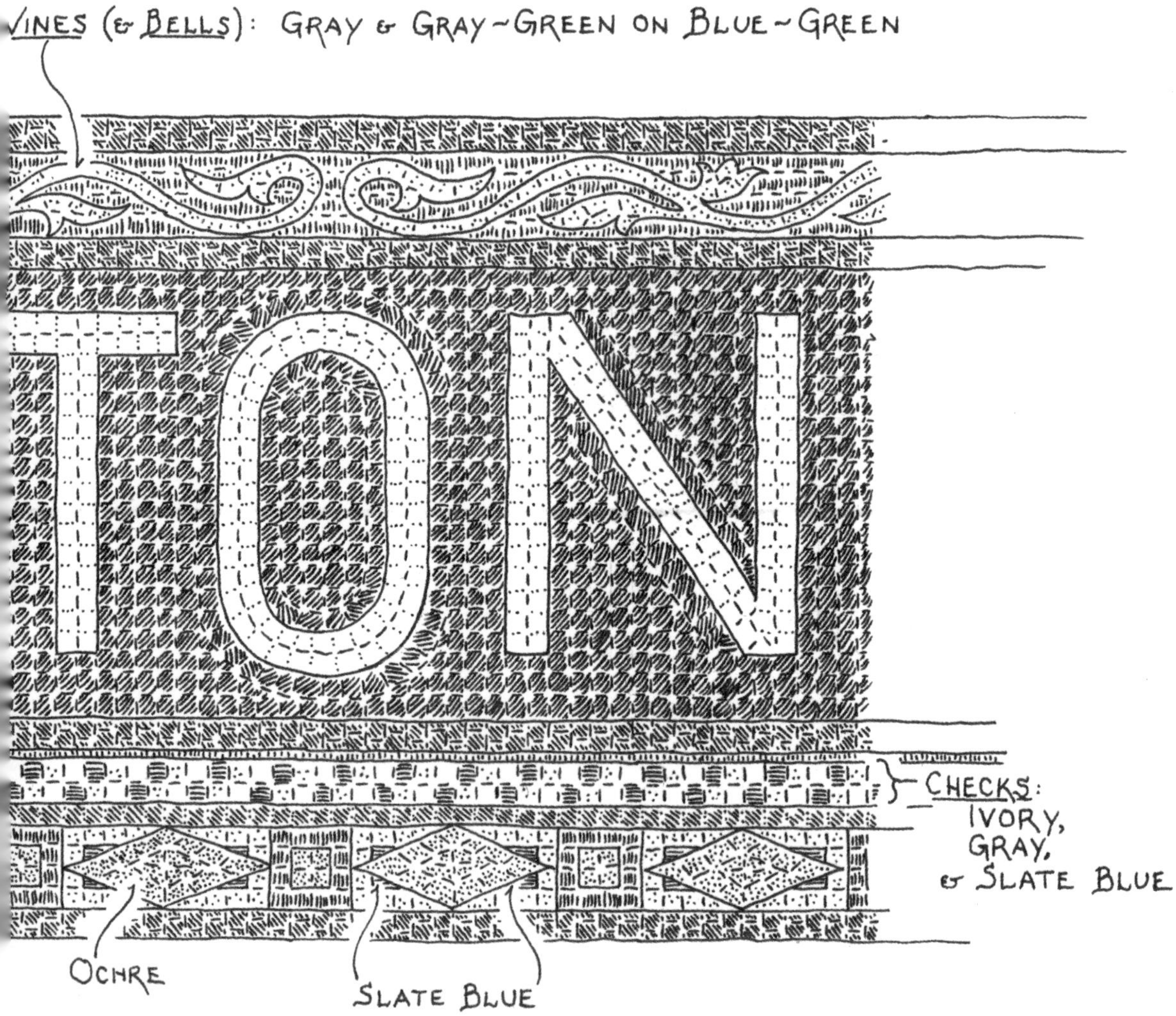

VINES (& BELLS): GRAY & GRAY~GREEN ON BLUE~GREEN

TON

CHECKS:
IVORY,
GRAY,
& SLATE BLUE

OCHRE

SLATE BLUE

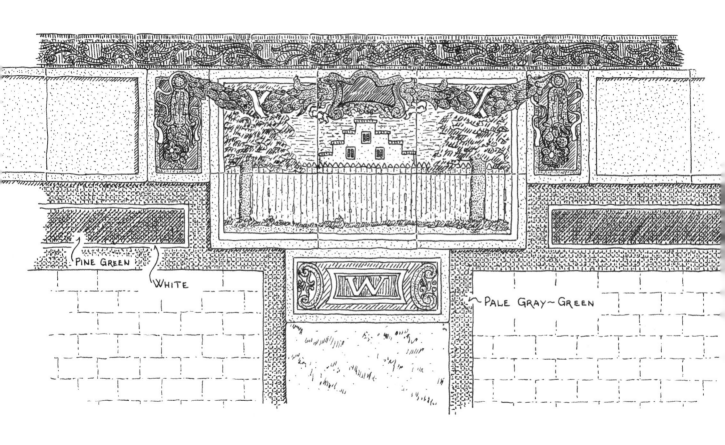

PINE GREEN

WHITE

PALE GRAY~GREEN

Wall Street
Faience plaque
4/5 lines

WALL STREET FAIENCE

Anyone seeing this view of Nieuw Amsterdam would have been standing just outside the Dutch settlement's limits, on the northern side of its fabled wall, which spanned the width of Manhattan isle. The Dutch Governor, Pieter Stuyvesant, had this wall erected in about 1653 to protect the town, as the British were challenging the Dutch's hold on the New World and there was an ongoing conflict with the Weckquaesgeek tribe.

The Dutch brigade that patrolled the interior of the wall eventually wore a path through the grass, and this dirt lane became known as the "Waal Straat." When the British attacked in 1664, they came in from the Bay rather than the north, so the wall didn't help. They took possession of Nieuw Amsterdam and recrowned it New York City.

The faience plaque was crafted at Rookwood Faience, Cincinnati, Ohio, in 1905. It was possibly modeled by John Dee Wareham.

FESTOONS & HANGING BOUQUETS:
    GRAY~GREEN, WITH IVORY RIBANDS
CARTOUCH BOX:
    GREEN, WITH A GRAY~GREEN FRAME
WALL PLAQUE:
    FOREGROUND: YELLOW OCHRE
    GRASS: GREEN
    TREES: BROWN TRUNKS, PINE GREEN BOUGHS
    WALL: RAW SIENNA PALLISADES, WITH PALE GREEN TIPS
    BUILDING: YELLOWISH
    WINDOWS: DULL BROWN, WITH PALE GREEN FRAMES
    SKY: MED. COBALT

Wall Street
Faience panel,
mosaics, and brick
4/5 lines

[No Cornice; Only Ceiling Above Here]

IVORY YELLOW
BABY BLUE
MED. COBALT
IVORY YELLOW
BABY BLUE

BABY BLUE
IVORY~YELLOW
BABY BLUE

PLEASANT GREEN
IVORY~YELLOW
PALE BLUE
MED. COBALT
IVORY~YELLOW

right:
Wall Street
Plaster beam strip
4/5 lines

below:
Wall Street
Faience panel,
mosaics, and brick
4/5 lines

Floral Frieze Cornice - Cobalt, with Ivory Roses
Reverse Bouquets - Iron Green

 = Column-into-Wall Iron Brace

BOWLING GREEN

The Bowling Green mosaic name panel was designed by LaFarge, rather late in the process of the project, and its name comes from the city's very first park, which sits above the station. Bowling Green's mosaic name panels were like no others in the entire subway system, but unfortunately, they're no longer with us. The MTA revamped the station from top to bottom in the late 70s, and not one of its beautiful mosaic name or rug panels was preserved.

The mosaics were composed by Felix Alcan and his European craftsmen in 1905.

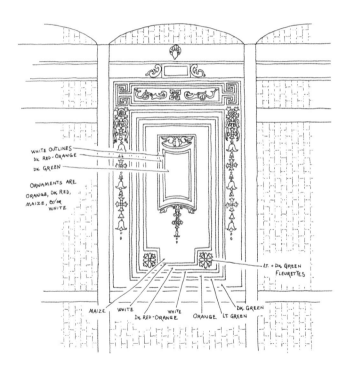

WHITE OUTLINES
DK. RED-ORANGE
DK. GREEN

ORNAMENTS ARE
ORANGE, DK. RED,
MAIZE, &/OR
WHITE

LT. + DK. GREEN
FLEURETTES

MAIZE   WHITE   WHITE   ORANGE LT. GREEN   DK. GREEN
DK. RED-ORANGE

Bowling Green
Mosaic panel
4/5 lines
(no longer visible)

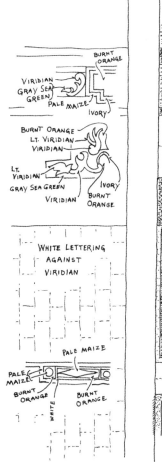

ORANGE

VIRIDIAN

GRAY

OCHRE
VIRIDIAN

BURNT
ORANGE

VIRIDIAN
GRAY SEA
GREEN
PALE MAIZE
IVORY

BURNT ORANGE
LT. VIRIDIAN
VIRIDIAN

LT.
VIRIDIAN
GRAY SEA GREEN   IVORY
VIRIDIAN   BURNT
ORANGE

PALE MAIZE
IVORY
BURNT ORANGE

WHITE LETTERING
AGAINST
VIRIDIAN

VIRIDIAN
GRAY VIRIDIAN
IVORY
GRAY SEA GREEN

VIRIDIAN

BOWLING GREEN

PALE MAIZE
BURNT ORANGE
CHECKS:
VIRIDIAN, &
GRAY SEA GREEN

PALE MAIZE

PALE
MAIZE
BURNT
ORANGE   BURNT
ORANGE
WHITE

Bowling Green
Mosaic name panel
4/5 lines
(no longer visible)

SOUTH FERRY

With wind whipping sharply across New York Bay, the Battery has always been a great place to sail. The Dutch held races here in sloops just like the one depicted in this station's plaques. In fact these sturdy little vessels were used to ferry people and cargo up the Hudson, monopolizing river traffic from the 1620s to nearly the 1850s, when paddleboats came to dominate the waterways.

These faience plaques have the deepest relief of all the system's pictorial décor. The porters hated them because so much dust settled on the sloop's hull and sails, requiring additional cleaning.

These faience plaques were fabricated at Hartford Faience, Connecticut, 1905. The master casting form was probably carved by Louis F. Dettenborn's woodworking company, which made models for various industries in the region.

"SF" PANEL:
  "SF" ~ PALE GREEN, AGAINST VERMILLION
  FRAME ~ OCHRE
  CURLY BRACKETS ~ PALE GREEN, AGAINST YELLOW
  ENFRAMING BARS (TOP & BOTTOM) ~ OCHRE
FESTOONS:
  BASICALLY YELLOW, WITH IVORY RIBANDS
  GREEN FLORAL ENDS
  YELLOW & WHITE FASTENING KNOBS
HANGING BOUQUETS:
  YELLOW, WITH WHITE RIBANDS, AGAINST VERMILLION
SLOOP PLAQUE:
  SEA ~ VIRIDIAN, WITH YELLOWER VIRIDIAN HIGHLIGHTS
  SKY ~ BLUE
  LAND ~ MAROON
  CLOUDS ~ WHITE, WITH MAROON SHADOWS
  HULL & MAST & LINES ~ RAW SIENNA
  SAILS & SEAGULL ~ WHITE
  DUTCHMAN ~ BLUE & IVORY

Color Scheme
South Ferry
Faience sloop plaque
1 line
(no longer visible)

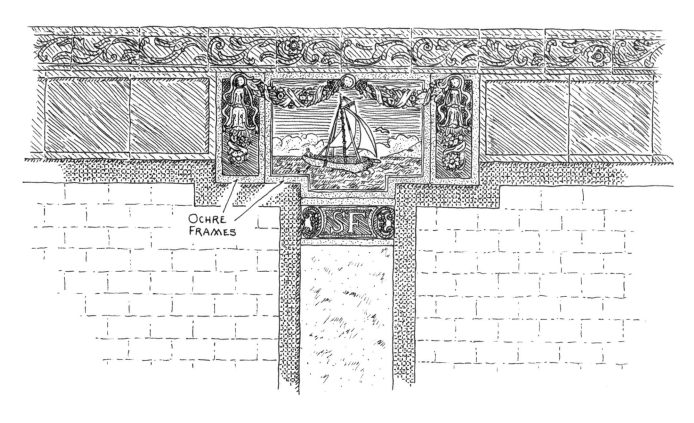

OCHRE
FRAMES

South Ferry
Faience sloop plaque
1 line
(no longer visible)

Borough Hall
Mosaic name panel
2/3/4/5 lines

BOROUGH HALL MOSAIC NAME PANEL

For this grand station, one of the jewels of the system and the IRT's first stop into Brooklyn, LaFarge fully celebrates his Beaux-Arts training in the design of the signage and décor. There is noble Roman capital lettering in the two bronze plaques at entrance level, set in broad panels replete with mosaic pilasters, festoons, fruits and flowers, ribbands, and ovoids. Downstairs there are gold-rimmed plates, ribbands, cascading florals, rosettes, fleurettes, motifs of egg and acanthus and bead and reel, consoles, and the majestic "BH" monogram plaques, set within a victor's wreath of laurel leaves and berries. Only one other station, 14th Street / Union Square, bore wreath plaques, but there they were entombed behind walls around 1910. Thankfully, we can still appreciate these Borough Hall splendors, as they have survived in full view for more than a century now.

The "BH" plaques and cornice were produced by Hartford Faience, Hartford, Connecticut, in 1908. The Dettenborn company probably crafted the casting master.

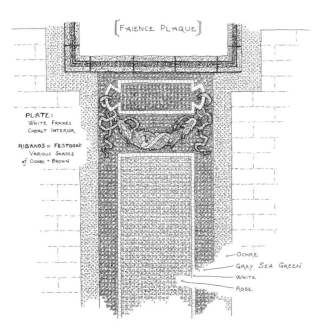

[FAIENCE PLAQUE]

PLATE:
WHITE FRAMES;
COBALT INTERIOR

RIBANDS & FESTOON:
VARIOUS SHADES
of OCHRE + BROWN

— OCHRE
— GREY SEA GREEN
— WHITE
— ROSE

below:
Borough Hall
Mosaic pilasters
2/3/4/5 lines

opposite:
Borough Hall
Mosaic setting for
bronze tablet
2/3/4/5 lines

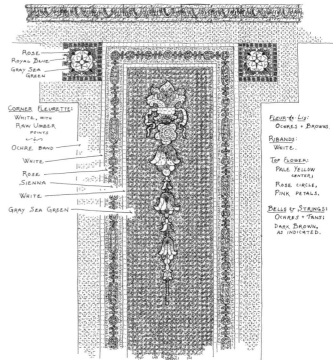

ROSE
ROYAL BLUE
GRAY SEA
GREEN

CORNER FLEURETTE:
WHITE, WITH
RAW UMBER
POINTS
&
OCHRE BAND

WHITE

ROSE
SIENNA

WHITE

GRAY SEA GREEN

FLEUR-de-LIS:
OCHRES + BROWNS.

RIBANDS:
WHITE.

TOP FLOWER:
PALE YELLOW
CENTER;
ROSE CIRCLE,
PINK PETALS.

BELLS & STRINGS:
OCHRES + TANS;
DARK BROWN,
AS INDICATED.

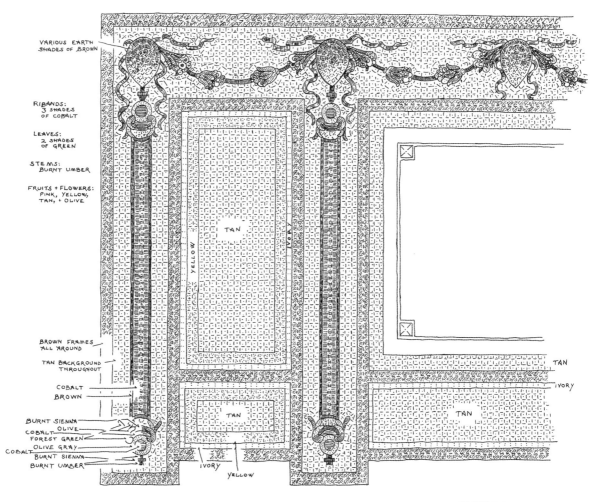

VARIOUS EARTH
SHADES OF BROWN

RIBANDS:
3 SHADES
OF COBALT

LEAVES:
2 SHADES
OF GREEN

STEMS:
BURNT UMBER

FRUITS + FLOWERS:
PINK, YELLOW,
TAN, + OLIVE

BROWN FRAMES
ALL AROUND

TAN BACKGROUND
THROUGHOUT

COBALT
BROWN

BURNT SIENNA
OLIVE
COBALT
FOREST GREEN
OLIVE GRAY
COBALT
BURNT SIENNA
BURNT UMBER

YELLOW

TAN

IVORY

IVORY

YELLOW

TAN

TAN

TAN

IVORY

TAN

GRAY-BEIGE CONSOLE:
GREEN   YELLOW, WHITE CENTER

GREEN;
FRUITS: RED, YELLOW, BROWN, OCHRE

OCHRE

BROWN BKGND;
PINK & ROSE PETALS,
PINK CENTER, BLACK SPIKES

SIENNA

— CHALK BLUE

SIENNA

IVORY-TAN

IVORY-TAN

ꓷROUGH HAᒪ

"BH": White,
Against Shiny Blue,
Within A Sienna Circle.

Wreath: Golden Ochre.

Central Flower: White,
With Sepia Leaves.

Corner Flowers: White,
Against Green Leaves.

Ribands: White.

Frame: Sienna.

opposite:
Borough Hall
Mosaic name panel
detail
2/3/4/5 lines

right:
Borough Hall
Faience monogram
plaque
2/3/4/5 lines

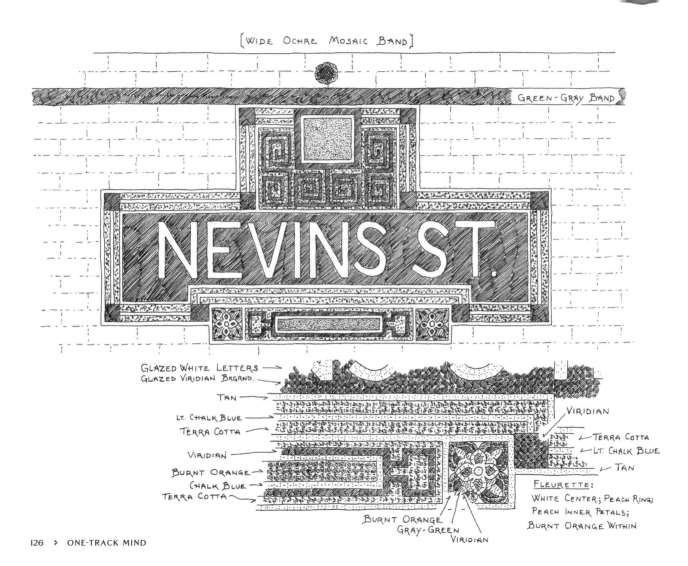

[WIDE OCHRE MOSAIC BAND]

GREEN-GRAY BAND

NEVINS ST.

GLAZED WHITE LETTERS
GLAZED VIRIDIAN BKGRND.

TAN

LT. CHALK BLUE
TERRA COTTA

VIRIDIAN

BURNT ORANGE
CHALK BLUE
TERRA COTTA

VIRIDIAN

TERRA COTTA
LT. CHALK BLUE

TAN

FLEURETTE:
WHITE CENTER; PEACH RING;
PEACH INNER PETALS;
BURNT ORANGE WITHIN

BURNT ORANGE
GRAY-GREEN
VIRIDIAN

BUFF →

VIRIDIAN

PLAQUE:
BUFF FRAME
GREEN VIRIDIAN BACKGROUND
IVORY INITIAL "N"

opposite:
Nevins Street
Faience plaque
2/3/4/5 lines
(no longer visible)

above:
Nevins Street
Mosaic name panel
2/3/4/5 lines

CREAM-BUFF CORNICE, PLAQUE FRAME, CARTOUCHE FRAME, & TULIPS

ROSE

INITIAL "A": IVORY,
AGAINST A GREEN VIRIDIAN BKGRND.

Atlantic Avenue
Faience plaque
2/3/4/5/LIRR lines

ATLANTIC AVENUE MOSAIC PLAQUE

This station is as far as the IRT's first line into Brooklyn reached. This "A" plaque, a typical design format found in many of the early IRT stops, features a round shield with embossed tulips flanking the station's initial. The plaque also bears a swastika fret pattern flowing to the cornice. One theory suggests that the ubiquity of tulips in much of the early subway's ceramic is a reference to New York's Dutch heritage.

Perhaps the faience "A" plaques are by Hartford Faience, which also produced the Borough Hall wreath plaques. The mosaic renditions of these plaques were likely fabricated by Felix Alcan.

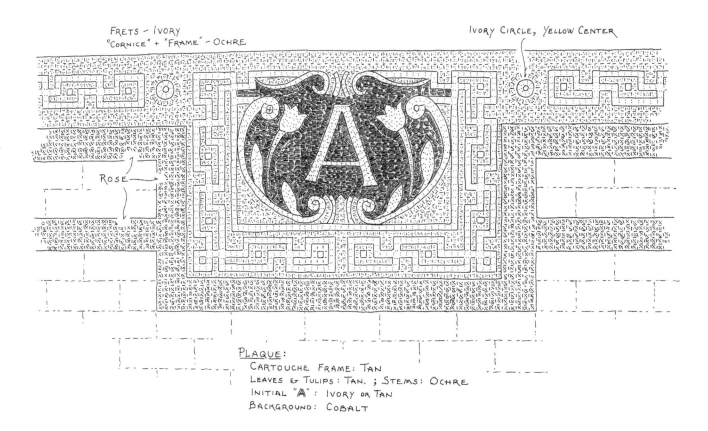

FRETS - IVORY
"CORNICE" + "FRAME" - OCHRE

IVORY CIRCLE, YELLOW CENTER

ROSE

PLAQUE:
CARTOUCHE FRAME: TAN
LEAVES & TULIPS: TAN. ; STEMS: OCHRE
INITIAL "A": IVORY OR TAN
BACKGROUND: COBALT

Atlantic Avenue
Mosaic name panel
2/3/4/5/LIRR lines

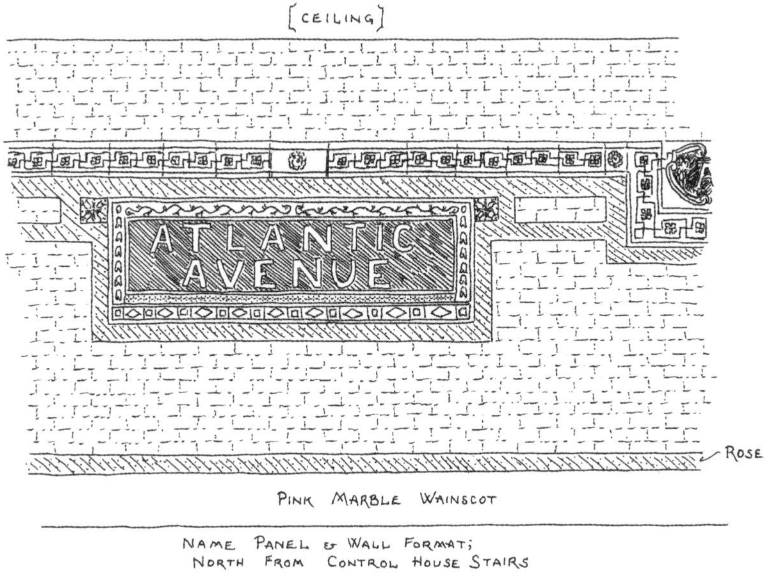

[CEILING]

CORNER FLEURETTES:
PALE GREY-BLUE BELLS,
SEPIA + SIENNA CROSS;
SLATE BLUE-GREEN BKGRND.

ATLANTIC
AVENUE

ROSE

ROSE

PINK MARBLE WAINSCOT

NAME PANEL & WALL FORMAT;
NORTH FROM CONTROL HOUSE STAIRS

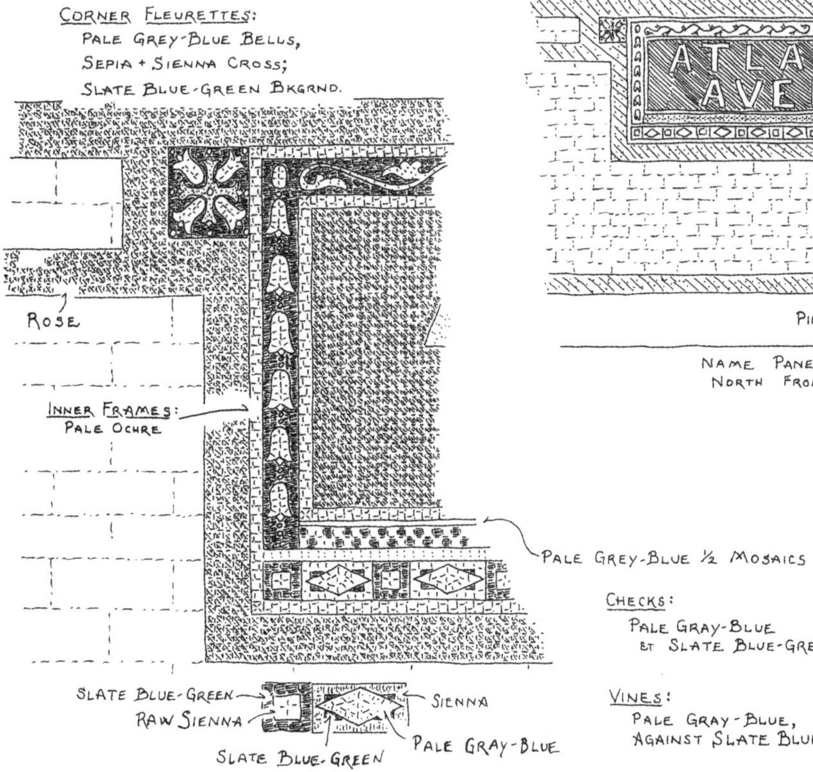

INNER FRAMES:
PALE OCHRE

PALE GREY-BLUE ½ MOSAICS

CHECKS:
PALE GRAY-BLUE
& SLATE BLUE-GREEN

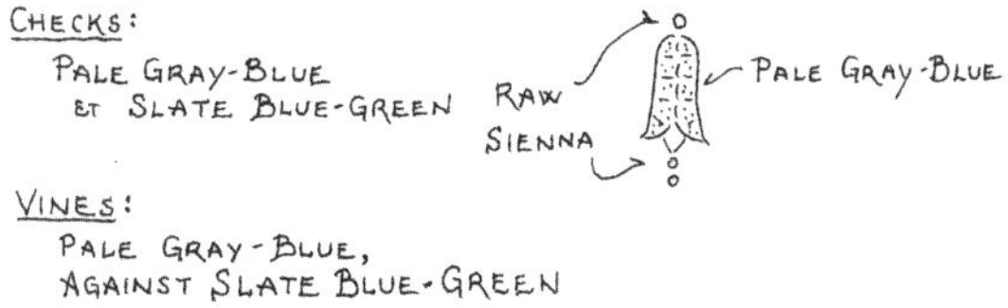

RAW
SIENNA

PALE GRAY-BLUE

VINES:
PALE GRAY-BLUE,
AGAINST SLATE BLUE-GREEN

SLATE BLUE-GREEN
RAW SIENNA

SIENNA

SLATE BLUE-GREEN

PALE GRAY-BLUE

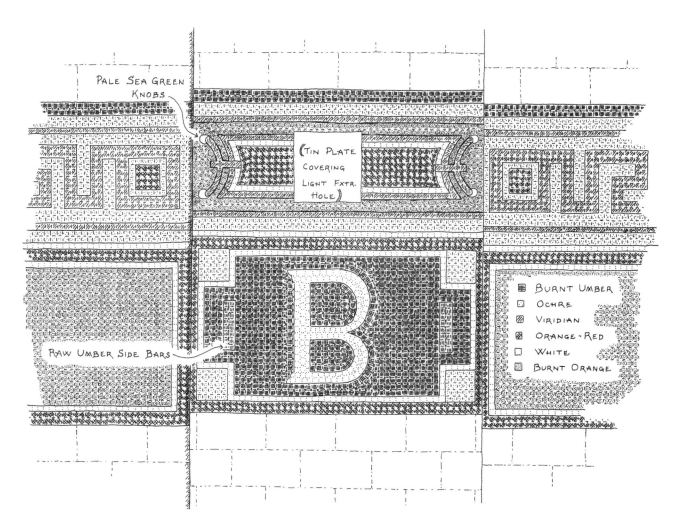

PALE SEA GREEN KNOBS

(TIN PLATE COVERING LIGHT FXTR. HOLE)

RAW UMBER SIDE BARS

▦ BURNT UMBER
▫ OCHRE
▨ VIRIDIAN
▨ ORANGE-RED
☐ WHITE
▨ BURNT ORANGE

opposite:
Bowery
Mosaic band
J/Z lines

below:
Bowery entrance
house
Mosaic design
J/Z lines
House demolished
(no longer visible)

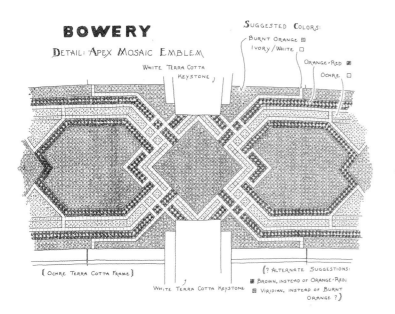

BOWERY

DETAIL: APEX MOSAIC EMBLEM

WHITE TERRA COTTA KEYSTONE)

SUGGESTED COLORS:
BURNT ORANGE ▨
IVORY/WHITE ☐
ORANGE-RED ▨
OCHRE ☐

[OCHRE TERRA COTTA FRAME]

WHITE TERRA COTTA KEYSTONE

(? ALTERNATE SUGGESTIONS:
▨ BROWN, INSTEAD OF ORANGE-RED;
▨ VIRIDIAN, INSTEAD OF BURNT ORANGE ?)

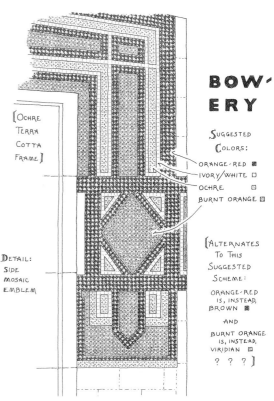

[OCHRE TERRA COTTA FRAME]

DETAIL: SIDE MOSAIC EMBLEM

BOW-ERY

SUGGESTED COLORS:
ORANGE-RED ▨
IVORY/WHITE ☐
OCHRE ☐
BURNT ORANGE ▨

[ALTERNATES TO THIS SUGGESTED SCHEME:

ORANGE-RED IS, INSTEAD, BROWN ▨
AND
BURNT ORANGE IS, INSTEAD, VIRIDIAN ▨
? ? ?]

BURNT UMBER

OCHRE

VIRIDIAN

TIN PLATE

TIN PLATE

VIRIDIAN

OCHRE

WHITE

ORANGE-RED

BURNT UMBER

WHITE

BURNT ORANGE

OCHRE

WHITE

below:
Cortlandt Street
Terracotta
ferryboat panel
1 line
(no longer visible)

GRAND CENTRAL FAIENCE
LOCOMOTIVE PLAQUE

When Grand Central Terminal's subway station opened in 1918, the locomotives depicted in these plaques were not contemporary to the times. They are bell-stacked locomotives from the 1860s, referencing the trains that Cornelius "Commodore" Vanderbilt built into his railroad empire and subsequent opening of his Grand Central Depot in 1871.

These faience plaques are probably the design work of Jay Van Everen, a friend of Squire J. Vickers, the chief designer of the Public Service Commission, and likely manufactured by the Herman Mueller Tile Company, of Trenton, New Jersey.

LOCOMOTIVE PLAQUE:
ENGINE = GRAYS + BROWNS
HEADLAMP = YELLOW
WINDOWS = BLUE + GREEN
COWCATCHER = GRAY
TRACK = GRAY; TIES = BROWN; OCHRE IN-BETWEEN
SEMAPHORES = GRAY POSTS, BLUE + RED ARMS
SKY = BLUES + GRAYS; HILLS = GREEN, GRAY, + SAND

Grand Central
Faience locomotive plaque
4/5/6 lines

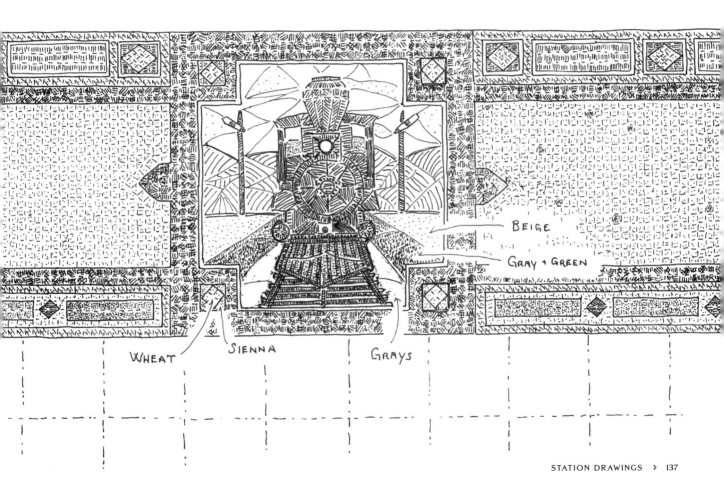

BEIGE

GRAY + GREEN

WHEAT

SIENNA

GRAYS

left:
Grand Central
Iron grilles
4/5/6 lines

below:
Grand Central
Mosaic pier band
4/5/6 lines

opposite:
Grand Central
Mosaic name panel
detail
4/5/6 lines

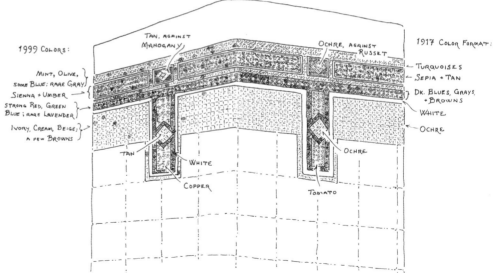

1999 COLORS:

MINT, OLIVE,
SOME BLUE; RARE GRAY

SIENNA + UMBER

STRONG RED, GREEN,
BLUE; RARE LAVENDER

IVORY, CREAM, BEIGE;
A FEW BROWNS

TAN, AGAINST
MAHOGANY

OCHRE, AGAINST
RUSSET

1917 COLOR FORMAT:

TURQUOISES

SEPIA + TAN

DK. BLUES, GRAYS,
+ BROWNS

WHITE

OCHRE

TAN

WHITE

COPPER

OCHRE

TOMATO

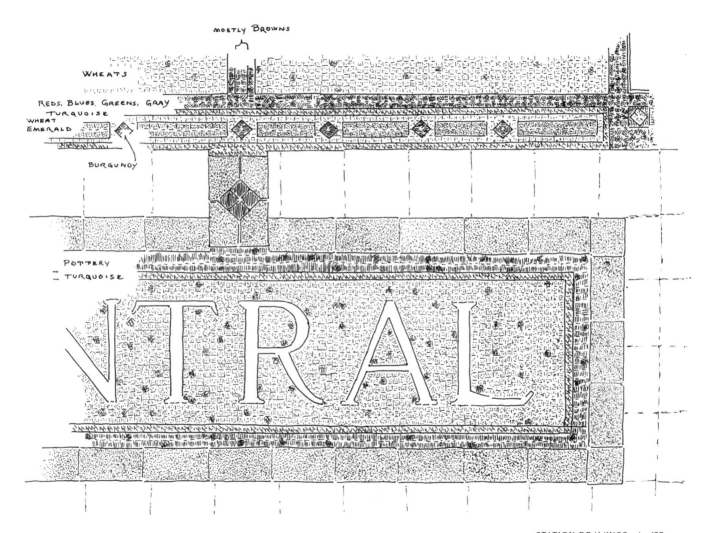

MOSTLY BROWNS

WHEATS

REDS, BLUES, GREENS, GRAY
TURQUOISE
WHEAT
EMERALD

BURGUNDY

POTTERY
TURQUOISE

NTRAL

86th Street
Mosaic band
4/5/6 lines

"86" ROUNDEL:
WHITE NUMERALS AGAINST BROWNS;
THIN WHITE INNER FRAME;
VIOLETS + VIRIDIANS OUTSIDE FRAME.

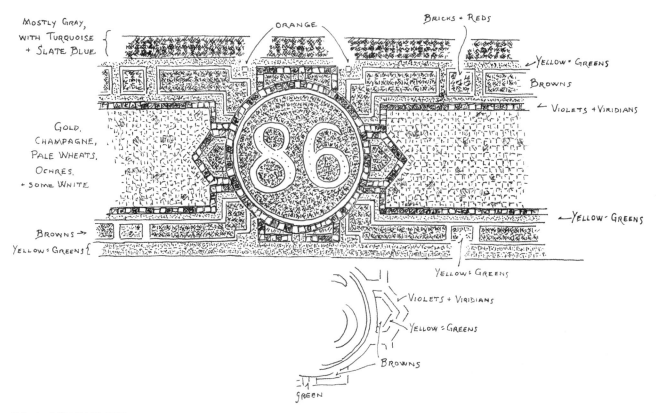

MOSTLY GRAY,
WITH TURQUOISE
+ SLATE BLUE

ORANGE

BRICKS + REDS

YELLOW-GREENS

BROWNS

← VIOLETS + VIRIDIANS

GOLD,
CHAMPAGNE,
PALE WHEATS,
OCHRES,
+ SOME WHITE

← YELLOW-GREENS

BROWNS →
YELLOW-GREENS

YELLOW-GREENS

VIOLETS + VIRIDIANS

YELLOW-GREENS

BROWNS

GREEN

Brooklyn Bridge
Circular ceiling wreath
4/5/6 lines
(no longer visible)

SKETCHBOOK

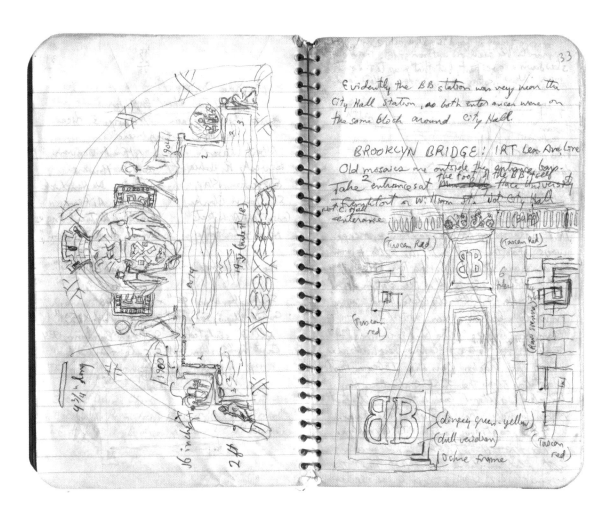

33

Evidently the BB station was very near the
City Hall station, so both entrances were on
the same block around City Hall.

BROOKLYN BRIDGE: IRT Lex Ave Line

Old mosaics are outside this entrance
The foot of the BB itself
Take 2 entrance at ~~~~ Place University
not C. Hall Frankfort or William St. Not City Hall
entrance

(Tuscan Red)   (Tuscan Red)

(Tuscan red)   6 ￼

(Rose ￼)

BB

(dingey green-yellow)   (Tuscan
(dull veridian)   red)
Ochre frame

9 3/4 in long
16 inches
2 ft
1906
193 (width 18)
1900

28th Street ✱ up & downtown

This station is really broken up. Original mosaics in central area of platform. Northern & southern extremes are low ceilinged and with the IND style tile arrangements. Colors are more harmonious. Mocha border, black frame, yellow frame, denim blue background tiles, white letters. Then, also, ~~some of~~ the walls from the token booth into the station are the new tan brick tiles. 50·4 3/4

The original walls reach very high and are in good condition. There is a difference in shade between the 3×6 tiles within the frames and outside them.

Blue egg + dart molding above all.

all faïence; no mosaics on this street sign. Bas relief

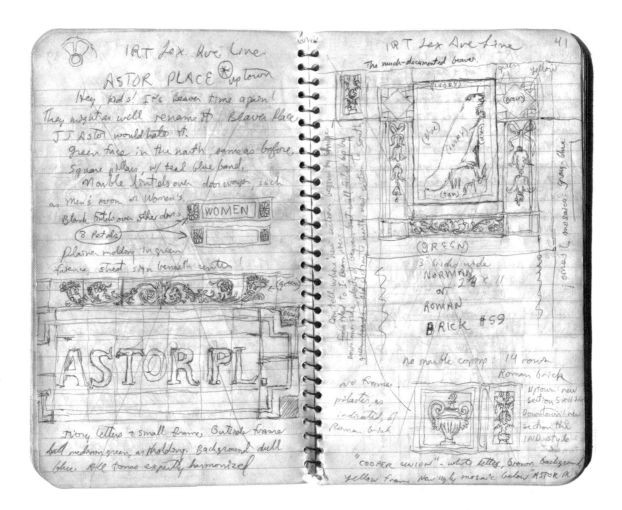

IRT Lex. Ave. Line

ASTOR PLACE ⊛ uptown

Hey kids! It's beaver time again!
They might as well rename it Beaver Place.
J.J. Astor would hate it.
   Green face in the north same as before.
Square pillars w/ teal blue band.
   Marble lintels over doorways, such
as Men's room or Women's.
Blank lintels over other doors.
(8 petals)

WOMEN

Plainer molding in green
Faience street sign beneath center!

(green)

ASTOR PL.

Ivory letters & small frame. Outside frame
dull medium green, or molding. Background dull
blue. All tones expertly harmonized.

IRT Lex Ave Line   41

The much-documented beaver.

(IVORY)   green   yellow

(blue)   (IVORY)
(tan)   (tan)

(GREEN)
3" bricks wide
NORMAN 2⅜ x 11
or
ROMAN
BRICK #59

no marble coping! 14 rows
                              Roman brick

no frames.
pilasters, as
indicated, of
Roman brick.

uptown: new
section S roll 41?
Downtown: new
section the
IND style?

"COOPER UNION" - white letters, brown background,
yellow frame. New ugly mosaic below "ASTOR P..."

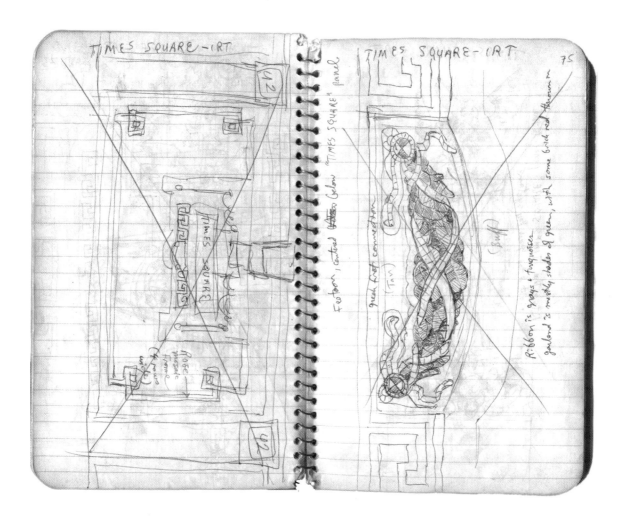

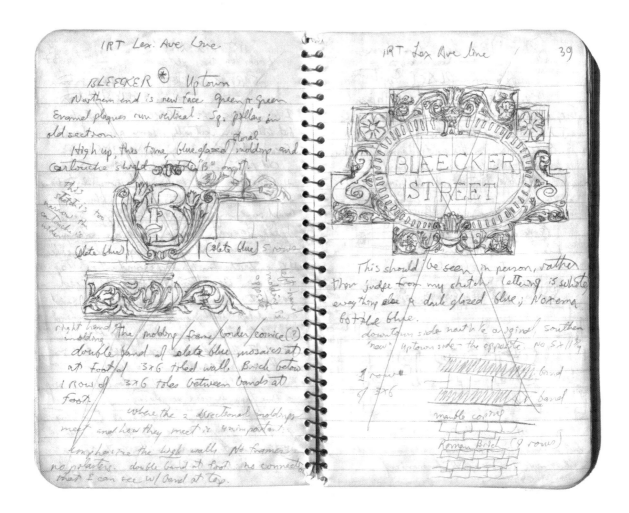

BLEECKER ✱ Uptown

Northern end is new face. Green + green
Enamel plaques run vertical. Sq. pillars in
old section.

High up, this time, blue glazed ↑floral molding and
Cartouche ↑shield ↑↑on "B" only?

This
sketch is too
narrow + the
cartouche is
not wide

(slate blue)   (slate blue) 5 rows

right hand ↑the molding / frame / border / cornice (?)
↑molding double band of slate blue mosaics at
at foot of 3x6 tiled walls. Brick below
1 row of 3x6 tiles between bands at
foot.

where the 2 directional moldings
meet and how they meet is unimportant.

Anywhere the high walls. No frames
no pilasters. double band at foot. No connection
that I can see w/ band at top.

BLEECKER
STREET

This should be seen in person, rather
than judge from my sketch. Lettering is white
everything else is dark glazed blue; Natrema
bottle blue.

downtown side north to be original. southern
"new". Uptown side - the opposite. No. 5 x 11 3/4

1 rows
of 3x6   band

                                          band

marble coping

Roman Brick (9 rows)

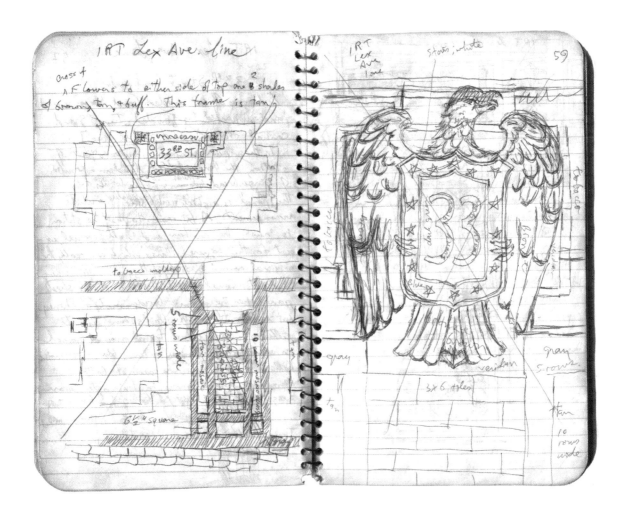

OVER 11'42" plagne

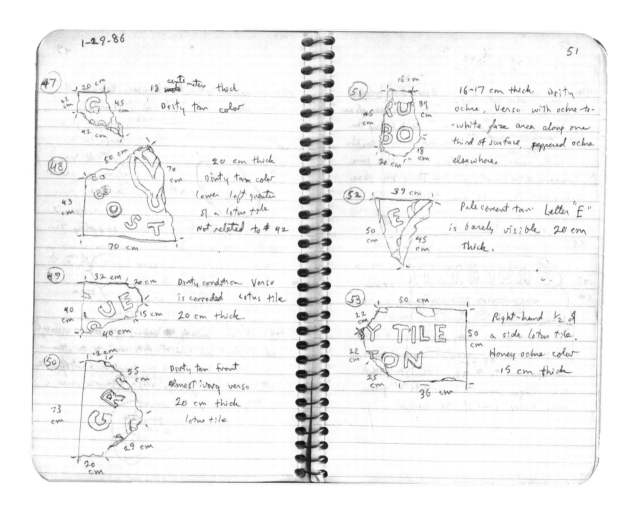

1-29-86

47. 20 cm / 32 cm / G / 45 cm / 42 cm

18 centimeter thick
Dirty tan color

48. 50 cm / 70 cm / 60 / 43 cm / O S T / 70 cm

20 cm thick
Dirty tan color
lower left quarter
of a lotus tile
Not related to #42

49. 32 cm / 20 cm / J E / 40 cm / 15 cm / 40 cm

Dirty condition. Verso
is corroded. Lotus tile
20 cm thick.

50. 12 cm / 55 cm / G R / 73 cm / G / 29 cm / 20 cm

Dirty tan front
Almost ivory verso
20 cm thick
lotus tile

51. 16 cm / R U / 39 cm / 45 cm / B O / 18 cm / 20 cm

16-17 cm thick. Dirty
ochre, Verso with ochre to-
-white glaze area along one
third of surface, peppered ochre
elsewhere.

52. 39 cm / E / 50 cm / 45 cm

Pale cement tan. Letter "E"
is barely visible. 20 cm
thick.

53. 50 cm / 22 cm / Y TILE / ON / 22 cm / 25 cm / 36 cm / 50 cm

Right-hand ½ of
a side lotus tile.
Honey ochre color
15 cm thick

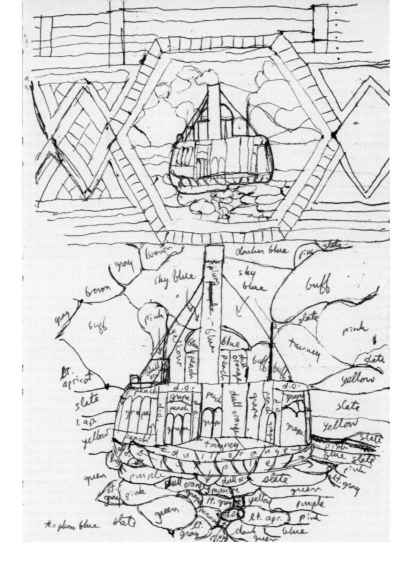

ACKNOWLEDGMENTS

I would like to thank the following people who have encouraged me, or advised me, or assisted me over the years. But I must acknowledge that this is not a complete list; there are so many that I'm not able to include. You have all been wonderful, and it's been a rewarding excursion. D. Chester Allen, Jr., Andrew Alpern (American Institute of Architects), Win Armstrong, David Barabbas (MTA), Rowland Bennett, David Black, Sandra Bloodworth (MTA), Ezra Bookstein, Joe Brennan, Frances S. Childs, Barbara Cohen (New York Bound Books), Justin Consalves and crew (CNN), David Roome Copp, Mary F. Roome Copp, Joseph A. Coppola, Joe Cunningham, David Dunlap (*New York Times*), Burton Fendelman, John Frazier (Urban Center), Larry Furlong (ERA), William Geist (*New York Times*), Cat Greenleaf, Thomas R. Jablonski (MTA), Dean Jones, Arnold B. Joseph (Railroadiana), Randy Kennedy (*New York Times*), Paul Kronenberg, Doug Martin (*New York Times*), Nym Korakot Punlopruksa, Yukie Ohta (New York Bound Books), Robert Peskin, David Pirmann, Catha Grace Rambusch, Sam Roberts (NY1), Carol Rubiano, Miho Sakai (NHK Television, Japan), Paul SanPietro (Transit Authority), Herbert Serious (New York Public Library), Judith Stonehill (New York Bound Books), Gilbert Tauber, Mary Antonia Thomas, Susan Tunick (Friends of Terra Cotta), Ruth Vickers, Mike Vincze, Linda Voorsanger, Kevin Walsh (Forgotten New York), Miles Ward (BBC), and Jeremy Workman.

—*Philip Ashforth Coppola*

We would like to thank Jonathan Lethem, Edward Burns, Robert Lyons, Austin Prario, Larry Walker, Jason Eppink, Matt Green, Denah S. Bookstein, Julia Malta-Weingard, Jose Martinez (NY1), Michael Miscione, Jeremiah Moss (Vanishing New York), Virgil Talaid (New York Transit Museum), Astrid von Ussar, Linda Zagaria, the General Society of Mechanics and Tradesmen, the National Arts Club, New York Transit Museum, Abby Bussel, Jennifer Lippert, Nina Pick, and everyone at Princeton Architectural Press.

—*Ezra Bookstein
and Jeremy Workman*

BIOGRAPHIES

Philip Ashforth Coppola is an artist and writer living in Somerset, New Jersey. He began drawing and researching the design elements of New York City subway stations in 1978, which he self-published in his encyclopedic *Silver Connections*. Coppola's artwork has been featured in the *New York Times* and *Hyperallergic*, among other print media. He is the subject of Jeremy Workman's award-winning documentary film *One Track Mind* (2005) and has been featured on multiple news outlets, including NHK World (Tokyo), WNBC, NY1, and on the BBC in conjunction with the one-hundredth anniversary of the New York City subway system. His work is part of the permanent collection of the National Arts Club; the Museum of Modern Art; the Science, Industry and Business branch of the New York Public Library; and other venues.

Jonathan Lethem is the author of *The Fortress of Solitude* and nine other novels. He lives in Los Angeles and Maine.

Jeremy Workman is a filmmaker living in New York City. He first met Philip Coppola in the early 2000s and became one of his closest friends. In 2005 he directed *One Track Mind*, a documentary about Coppola that premiered at the Tribeca Film Festival; it is included in the anthology documentary film *True New York* (First Run Features). In 2014 Workman directed the acclaimed documentary *Magical Universe* about outsider artist Al Carbee; released theatrically by IFC Films, the film is widely available on all platforms. A graduate of Columbia University, he is currently completing *Walk: 8000 Miles in New York*, a feature documentary on Matt Green and his mission to walk every street of New York City.

Ezra Bookstein is a filmmaker, sculptor, producer, and author living in New York City. He is the winner of an Emmy Award for documentary camerawork, and his feature documentary, *The Rich Have Their Own Photographers*, screened at film festivals worldwide, on PBS, and at the Getty Museum and British Museum, among many others. As creator of the Smith Tapes project, Bookstein produced the Grammy-nominated limited-edition box set, hundreds of hours of audio content, and the book, *The Smith Tapes: Lost Interviews with Rock Stars & Icons*, 1969–1972 (Princeton Architectural Press, 2015).

PHIL, JEREMY, AND EZRA WOULD LIKE TO THANK
THE ARTISTS, ARCHITECTS, AND CRAFTSMEN
WHOSE BEAUTIFUL WORK IN NEW YORK CITY'S
SUBWAY STATIONS STILL INSPIRES US, MORE THAN
A HUNDRED YEARS LATER.

THIS·TABLET·IS·ERECTED·TO
COMMEMORATE·THE·OPENING
OF·THE·FIRST·SUBWAY·UNITING
THE·BOROUGHS·OF·MANHATTAN
AND·BROOKLYN·JANUARY·9·1908